# THE MORMONS

# THE MORMONS

AN ILLUSTRATED HISTORY OF
**THE CHURCH OF JESUS CHRIST OF LATTER-DAY SAINTS**

**EDITED BY ROY A. PRETE**
ASSOCIATE EDITORS: RICHARD O. COWAN, JOHN P. LIVINGSTONE, CRAIG J. OSTLER

**MERRELL**
LONDON · NEW YORK

First published in 2013 by Merrell Publishers,
London and New York

Merrell Publishers Limited
81 Southwark Street
London SE1 0HX

merrellpublishers.com

A catalogue record for this book is available from the
Library of Congress.

ISBN 978-1-8589-4620-7

Cover and book design by Stephen Hales Creative, Inc.,
Provo, Utah.

Printed and bound in China

Front cover: Temple Square in Salt Lake City, Utah, at
dusk with the State Capitol building in the background,
Don Busath. Back cover: *Jesus Christ,* by Heinrich
Hoffman, C. Harrison Conroy Co. Inc.; Salt Lake Temple,
Val Brinkerhoff; all others © Intellectual Reserve, Inc.,
including missionaries, Matt Reir; *Joseph Smith,* by Alvin
Gittins; and family prayer, Cody Bell. Spine: Angel Moroni,
Skip Weeks. Dust jacket: door knob, Troy Roberts; Roy
and Carma Prete, Joseph Prete.

## Scriptural Abbreviations

### Holy Bible
Standard abbreviations

### Book of Mormon

| | |
|---|---|
| 1 Ne. | 1 Nephi |
| 2 Ne. | 2 Nephi |
| Jacob | Jacob |
| Enos | Enos |
| Jarom | Jarom |
| Omni | Omni |
| W of M | Words of Mormon |
| Mosiah | Mosiah |
| Alma | Alma |
| Hel. | Helaman |
| 3 Ne. | 3 Nephi |
| 4 Ne. | 4 Nephi |
| Morm. | Mormon |
| Ether | Ether |
| Moro. | Moroni |

### Doctrine and Covenants

| | |
|---|---|
| D&C | Doctrine and Covenants |
| OD | Official Declaration |

### Pearl of Great Price

| | |
|---|---|
| P of GP | Pearl of Great Price |
| Moses | Moses |
| Abr. | Abraham |
| JS–M | Joseph Smith—Matthew |
| JS–H | Joseph Smith—History |
| A of F | Articles of Faith |

*(Previous spread) Replica of the* Christus *statue by
Bertel Thorvaldson in the North Visitors' Center on
Temple Square, Salt Lake City, Utah.*

*(This spread) A family prepares to go camping.
Mormons are noted for the strength of their
family life.*

# Contents

Mormons are ordinary people, found every-where in the world where there is religious freedom.

# Preface

AS MORMONS BECOME MORE VISIBLE IN A variety of walks of life, many people are interested in learning the true nature of their beliefs and practices. This book offers a behind-the-scenes look at Mormons. It tells the story of Mormonism as seen through the eyes of those who practice it every day. For them it is more than a religion; it is a way of life! What better way to understand the Mormons?

Mormonism is a dynamic religious movement. Organized in upstate New York in 1830, The Church of Jesus Christ of Latter-day Saints (whose members prefer to be called "Latter-day Saints," but are commonly referred to as "Mormons" because of their belief in the Book of Mormon) is one of the fastest growing Christian churches in the world. Founded with six charter members, it has become the fourth largest religion in the United States, with six million members. In 1950 it was largely a North American church, with just 11 percent of its 1.3 million members outside the United States and Canada. Now, it has become a world religion found in 150 countries with a membership of over 14 million, nearly 60 percent of whom are outside the United States.

What is the cause of this phenomenal success? How does the Mormon Church profile in relationship to other Christian churches? Do its members follow the Bible? What are its core beliefs and values? What in fact makes Mormons tick? In their long history, Mormons have frequently been at odds with the mainstream of American life. Have those tensions been satisfactorily resolved? And, perhaps more importantly, since the Church has become more and more international, how do its members adapt to the widely differing cultures in which they live?

Who better to answer these questions than Mormons themselves? This volume, by a panel of experts in their fields—knowledgeable on the origin, history, beliefs, lifestyle, and dynamics of their religion, as well as its daily challenges—answers these questions and many more. This book, which is a pictorial introduction to The Church of Jesus Christ of Latter-day Saints and its people, appeals for its human interest and the superb quality of its imagery. But it is more. By focusing on the background, basic beliefs, and core values of this vigorous religious tradition, it lays the groundwork for understanding Mormonism.

## Acknowledgements

I am indebted to several persons and institutions in the preparation of this volume. The authors and editors are to be praised for their unstinted efforts. Associate editor Richard O. Cowan helped shape the study and author Helen Warner was a pillar of support. Master photographers Don Busath, Val Brinkerhoff, and Ed Thompson graciously gave access to their excellent collections. Many photographs were supplied by LDS Intellectual Reserve, Inc., in Salt Lake City, Utah; by Brigham Young University; by *Deseret News* and *Church News,* its weekly supplement; and by numerous other institutions and individuals mentioned in the credits. Kimberly Reid, Kay Stevenson, Stephanie Swift, Rachelle Price, and Thaya Gilmore rendered yeoman service. Stephen Hales designed the book, while editor Carlotta Lemieux added grace and clarity to the text. Judy Dunlop prepared the index. Family members were unfailingly supportive and provided useful advice and counsel. Lastly, I am grateful to my wife Carma for her constant support.

This book contains only the wisdom of its authors and does not represent the views of the publisher or the official position of The Church of Jesus Christ of Latter-day Saints.

**ROY A. PRETE**
**EDITOR**

# A Visit to Temple Square

**Lloyd D. Newell**

◄ *The Salt Lake Temple is the symbolic heart of The Church of Jesus Christ of Latter-day Saints worldwide. Positioned on Salt Lake City's center block, known as Temple Square, the Salt Lake Temple stands amid downtown high-rises, office buildings, and shopping malls. More important than its recognizable exterior, however, are eternal marriages and other sacred ordinances performed within its walls.*

JUST DAYS AFTER ARRIVING IN THE SALT LAKE VALLEY in July 1847, Brigham Young selected the site for the Salt Lake Temple. More than 150 years later, this spot is one of the most visited places in the United States, hosting some five million people a year. Historic Temple Square in downtown Salt Lake City, headquarters of The Church of Jesus Christ of Latter-day Saints, is known worldwide for its beautiful gardens and immaculately maintained buildings. It offers both a spiritual and historical oasis in the Utah desert.

There is much to see here: the magnificent Conference Center; the historic Assembly Hall; the FamilySearch Center; the Family History Library, the largest genealogical library in the world; the Church History Museum, housing a vast collection of Latter-day Saint artwork, photographs, and artifacts; and the notable Salt Lake Tabernacle, home to the renowned Mormon Tabernacle Choir.

Temple Square is open every day of the year for tours, available at no cost in more than 35 languages. If you visit, you will truly see and experience Mormon culture as you learn more about Mormon beliefs and Salt Lake City's rich pioneer heritage.

## The Salt Lake Temple

At the heart of Temple Square is the Salt Lake Temple. The fortress-like structure was built to symbolize strength and spiritual safety. The walls are nine feet thick at the base and six feet thick at the top. The quartz monzonite exterior, which looks like granite, comes from Little Cottonwood Canyon, located 20 miles (32 km) southeast of the temple site. Oxen transported the massive blocks during the early years of construction, until the Transcontinental Railroad was completed in 1869 and stones could be carried by rail at a much faster rate.

The Salt Lake Temple is the Church's largest temple. It took 40 years to build and stands today as a testament to the faith and perseverance of its pioneer builders. More important, it is a place of prayer, meditation, and worship. The temple is used by members of the Church in good standing for performing sacred ordinances and ceremonies, such as eternal marriage. Mormons believe that marriages and families can endure beyond the grave when covenants made in the temple are faithfully observed.

In temples, Latter-day Saints also perform other sacred ordinances, such as baptism on behalf of deceased ancestors

◄ *The temple's east center tower is capped by a statue of an angel announcing with a trump the restored gospel message to all the earth. A similar statue stands atop more than 130 Latter-day Saint temples around the world.*

(see 1 Cor. 15:29). They believe that God has commanded them to be "saviours . . . on mount Zion" (Obad. 1:21) by making these ordinances available to those who died without receiving them in mortality.

▲ Temple Square is noted for its beautiful and meticulously maintained gardens.

◀◀ The angel Moroni atop the central east tower of the Salt Lake Temple, captured in the moonlight.

◀ Life-size statues of Mormonism's founder, Joseph Smith (right), and his brother Hyrum stand on Temple Square. The brothers died together as martyrs for their faith.

▶ The Salt Lake Temple is a monument to the Mormon pioneers who sacrificed for 40 years to build it.

◀ *At the time of its construction, between 1863 and 1867, the Salt Lake Tabernacle was the largest auditorium in the nation without a center support. It remains an architectural and engineering wonder. The Tabernacle has seating capacity for nearly 3,000 and serves as a venerable gathering place for conferences, concerts, eminent speakers, and performing artists.*

▶ ▼ *The Tabernacle's organ is one of the world's most recognized musical instruments, accompanying the Tabernacle Choir on its weekly* Music and the Spoken Word *broadcast since 1929.*

## The Salt Lake Tabernacle

The Tabernacle is home to the world-renowned Mormon Tabernacle Choir and Orchestra at Temple Square. The Tabernacle is especially known for its dome shape and exceptional acoustic qualities. The unique vaulted ceiling makes it possible to hear speakers without the use of a microphone. In fact, if all present remain still, a pin dropped on the pulpit can be heard clearly in every part of the Tabernacle.

The oldest building on Temple Square, the Tabernacle has long been the home of the choir to which it gave its name—the Mormon Tabernacle Choir. For decades it was also the home of the Church's general conferences. With the exception of Joseph Smith, every President of the Church has spoken here—a historical continuity that stretches from the era of Brigham Young to the 21st century.

The construction of so unique a structure was an extraordinary endeavor of pioneer resourcefulness and ingenuity. The arches were made of timbers pegged together with wooden dowels that were split and wedged at each end. Cracked timbers were wrapped with moist rawhide, which contracted as it dried to make a tight binding. When finished, the roof was nine feet thick, and the plaster ceiling was 68 feet above the floor. The structure was an engineering wonder in its day, prompting Frank Lloyd Wright to later dub the Tabernacle "one of the architectural masterpieces of the country and perhaps the world."[1]

The Tabernacle's organ is one of the finest pipe organs ever built. The pipes were fashioned from tall, straight-grained pine that ox-drawn wagons hauled 300 miles to Salt Lake City. Since its completion, the organ has been renovated and enlarged several times by prominent organ companies.

However, the case is the original one, and many of the pipes—including the large, gilded front pipes and some pipes inside the case—are the same pipes that the oxen hauled so many years ago. Visitors can hear these famous pipes play during free daily recitals.

## The Mormon Tabernacle Choir

The official choir of The Church of Jesus Christ of Latter-day Saints is one of the best-known choirs in the world. It is composed of more than 360 carefully selected and well-trained vocalists who come from diverse backgrounds and professions, serve without pay, range in age from 25 to 60, and demonstrate great commitment in their volunteer service as they rehearse and perform more than 150 days each year. The choir is beloved worldwide for its many recordings and extensive tours, which have included performances in major concert halls throughout North America, Europe, Central America, Australia, Asia, and the former Soviet Union, to name a few. Five of the choir's recordings have achieved gold-record status, and two have gone platinum. "The Battle Hymn of the Republic," a 1959 recording with Eugene Ormandy and the Philadelphia Orchestra, won a Grammy Award.

The Mormon Tabernacle Choir has become part of the American cultural landscape. It was designated by US President George H. W. Bush as "one of America's greatest treasures," and by President Ronald Reagan as "America's Choir." The choir has performed at five presidential inaugurations and on other national occasions, including a broadcast following the 9/11 terrorist attack; the opening ceremonies of the 2002 Winter Olympics, seen by 3.5 billion people; the bicentennial of the United States Constitution; radio memorial services for Franklin D. Roosevelt and John F. Kennedy; and the first worldwide television satellite broadcast, transmitted from Mount Rushmore in 1962.

Since 1929, the choir has been heard "from the crossroads of the West" on its weekly broadcast, *Music and the Spoken Word,* which is carried today around the world by some 2,000 radio, television, and cable stations. It is the longest continuous nationwide network broadcast in the world. The program twice received the Peabody Award for service to American Broadcasting, was twice awarded the Freedom Foundation's George Washington Award, and received the National Medal of Arts. In April 2004, *Music and the Spoken Word* was inducted into the National Association of Broadcasters Hall of Fame, one of only two radio programs to be so inducted, and in November 2010, by a vote of the American listening public, *Music and the Spoken Word* was inducted into the National Radio Hall of Fame. These recognitions affirm the cultural significance of the choir's broadcast. In a world so strident and full of distraction, *Music and the Spoken Word* is a welcome reprieve. Through world wars and times of peace, through prosperity and depression, this program of music and message "from within the shadows of the everlasting hills" gently reminds listeners of life's purposes.[2]

The Orchestra at Temple Square is an all-volunteer orchestra, organized in 1999, that functions as a concert orchestra as well as accompanying the choir on their weekly broadcast, concert tours, and other special events.

The Tabernacle Choir performs *Music and the Spoken Word* each Sunday at 9:30 a.m. (mountain time) and rehearses on Thursdays at 8:00 p.m. Both are free and open to the public.

▲ *The Mormon Tabernacle Choir in front of St. Basil's Cathedral in Moscow, during a 1991 tour shortly after the fall of the Iron Curtain. Part of the choir's mission is to serve as an ambassador of goodwill in tours to many locations throughout the world.*

▶ *The Mormon Tabernacle Choir and Orchestra at Temple Square perform in the historic Tabernacle.*

*(Overleaf) A Christmas concert featuring the Mormon Tabernacle Choir and Orchestra at Temple Square, and other performing groups, is presented each year as a gift to the community and nation. All four performances are free to the public, and the 21,000-seat Conference Center is filled to capacity each night. The annual concert has become the most watched Christmas program on PBS stations nationwide.*

▶ *The Church Office Building towers over the Church Administration Building, symbolizing the growth of the Church into a global organization.*

▶▶ *Interior of the Conference Center*

## The Church Office and Administration Buildings

The Church Office Building is Salt Lake City's tallest structure (28 floors above ground, three levels below), and is the home of the day-to-day operations of the Church. Built in the early 1970s, this building stands as a symbol of the growth of the Church from its pioneer beginnings to the worldwide organization it is today. The Church Office Building observation deck is open to the public free of charge, Monday through Friday, and provides a good view of the city, the Great Salt Lake, the Wasatch and Oquirrh Mountains, and Temple Square.

The Church Administration Building, constructed from 1914 to 1917, houses the offices of the First Presidency and the Quorum of the Twelve Apostles, the Church's highest governing bodies. The building is open only to Church officials and their guests.

## The Conference Center

The Conference Center is one of the largest indoor auditoriums in the world, seating 21,000 in the main assembly hall. There are no pillars supporting the two balconies; they are supported entirely by cantilevers, allowing all 21,000 seats an unobstructed view of the podium. A Boeing 747 airplane could easily fit inside the auditorium, yet the spacious hall has been designed so that those in attendance can hear the speakers and music clearly.

The Conference Center covers 10 acres and is 1.5 million square feet inside. The enormous structure was built to the highest seismic codes, the latest in architectural and engineering technology, and state-of-the-art broadcasting capabilities. It took three large construction companies and

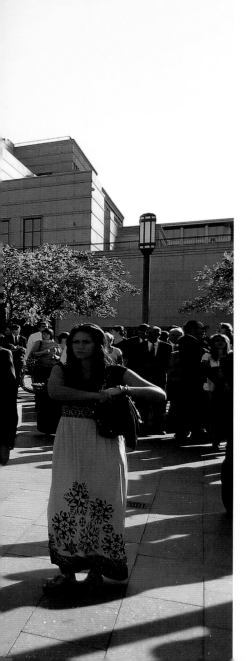

80 subcontractors to handle the mammoth project. Often a thousand workers were at the site each day.

The Conference Center's roof is landscaped with a waterway, trees, shrubs, and grasses to blend into the surroundings and complement the majestic Salt Lake Temple.

Like the Tabernacle to the south, the Conference Center is primarily a place of worship and gospel instruction. However, uplifting cultural events, concerts, and pageants are also held here. Guided tours are available daily at no cost.

*◄ ▼ ► Some of the Conference Center's notable features include fountains, beautiful art and finishing work, a custom-built organ with over 7,600 pipes, and translation facilities for more than 80 languages. The entire podium can be moved for stage productions, as was done during the 2002 Winter Olympics.*

### The Assembly Hall

The Assembly Hall is a gothic-style building with 40 beautiful stained-glass windows and 130-foot spires. The interior panels are adorned with carvings of beehives, sego lilies, and sheaves of grain, meaningful symbols to its pioneer builders. Construction spanned 1877 to 1882, and because 1880 was the 50th anniversary of the founding of the Church, builders included the Star of David in the structure, in honor of the Old Testament custom of a "jubilee" celebration every 50 years (see Lev. 25:8–10).

### North and South Visitors' Centers

Visitors' centers on Temple Square are designed to convey the message of the gospel of Jesus Christ, highlight the importance of the family as well as the Church's welfare and humanitarian aid efforts, and explain the teachings and history of The Church of Jesus Christ of Latter-day Saints. They feature short films, interactive displays and beautiful artwork, as well as many places to sit and ponder.

### The Family History Library

The Family History Library is the largest genealogical library in the world. It houses records from over 100 countries and offers record translation in about 30 languages. Free of charge, visitors can browse the library's vast resources, take classes, or consult with expert genealogists (see Chapter 12).

### The Church History Museum

Next door to the Family History Library is the Church History Museum. Artwork, photos, and artifacts make up the museum's permanent and temporary exhibits, showcasing almost two centuries' worth of Latter-day Saint history.

▲ *On the southwest corner of Temple Square stands the Assembly Hall, completed in 1882. Like the Salt Lake Temple, it was built of quartz monzonite rock, taken from the same quarry. The charming gothic-style building is used for free musical concerts that are held on Friday and Saturday evenings.*

▲ *The visitors' centers on Temple Square feature a number of paintings depicting the life of the Savior.*

▶ *The North Visitors' Center at dusk. A large replica of Bertel Thorvaldson's statue* Christus *is featured in the rotunda.*

## The Joseph Smith Memorial Building

The impressive Joseph Smith Memorial Building began its life as the Hotel Utah, one of the finest hotels west of the Mississippi River. The hotel opened for business in 1911 and hosted dignitaries from around the world, Latter-day Saint conference-goers, conventioneers, tourists, skiers, and every US president since William Howard Taft in 1912. No longer a hotel, the Joseph Smith Memorial Building is now a National Historic Site. It houses a chapel, two rooftop restaurants, offices, a theater that shows movies about Jesus Christ and the history of the Church, facilities for special events, and the FamilySearch Center, which contains more than 200 computers along with staff to assist visitors in filling out their family trees.

▲ *The magnificent entry area of the Joseph Smith Memorial Building was once the lobby of the Hotel Utah, which was built between 1909 and 1911. The hotel operated until 1987, when it underwent major renovations and in 1995 it was opened as the Joseph Smith Memorial Building.*

▶ *The Joseph Smith Memorial Building includes two rooftop restaurants that give a magnificent view of Salt Lake City.*

▶ ▶ *The Joseph Smith Memorial Building, located just east of the Salt Lake Temple, blends in with the cityscape of downtown Salt Lake City. It houses a theater, the FamilySearch Center, offices, restaurants, a chapel, and other facilities.*

### Notes

1. Carrie A. Moore, "What's Changed at Tabernacle?" *Deseret News,* March 27, 2007.

2. For more information about the Mormon Tabernacle Choir, see Charles J. Calman, *The Mormon Tabernacle Choir* (New York: Harper and Row, 1979); Richard L. Evans, Jr., *Richard L. Evans: The Man and the Message* (Salt Lake City: Bookcraft, 1973); and Heidi Swinton, *America's Choir* (Salt Lake City: Shadow Mountain, 2004). For more information on the choir's history and accolades, see Lisa Ann Jackson, "From the Crossroads of the West," *Ensign,* July 2004, 68–73. See also Terryl Givens, *People of Paradox* (Oxford University Press, 2007), Chapter 13, which situates the choir in the context of both LDS culture and the broader culture and discusses the public perception and national appeal of the choir.

# Salt Lake City and Utah

**Craig J. Ostler and John P. Livingstone**

◄ *The recently completed City Creek Center is a two-billion-dollar renovation of downtown Salt Lake City that begins immediately south of Temple Square. It offers high-end retail enterprises under a retracting glass roof, as well as fine condominium and apartment living spaces in the very heart of the city.*

▼ *A monument to the seagull, the Utah State Bird, rests on Temple Square, reminding local residents of the miraculous appearance of hordes of gulls which attacked and ate crickets infesting pioneer crops and saved the populace from starvation in the early days of the founding of Salt Lake City.*

WHEN BRIGHAM YOUNG AND THE FIRST COMPANY OF 148 Mormon settlers entered the Salt Lake Valley in late July 1847—having just trekked nearly a thousand miles from Omaha, Nebraska—they found an arid wasteland. The hardy pioneers immediately set to work, damming the streams and diverting water onto the land. This foundation of ongoing irrigation eventually made the desert "blossom as the rose" (Isa. 35:1).

One of the great colonizers of all time, Brigham Young established more than 350 Mormon colonies in the Intermountain West, mainly in Utah, Idaho, and Nevada. The largest of these settlements was Salt Lake City, which by 1849 had developed into a thriving community of 4,000. By 2012, the population of Salt Lake City and surrounding area had reached 1.2 million.

The city, nestled at the feet of the towering Wasatch Mountains, has a unique layout. Joseph Smith had drawn a plan for "a city of Zion," with a temple at its center and very wide streets spreading out north-south and east-west. Brigham Young followed this plan when laying out Salt Lake City and all other new cities in Mormon settlements. Known as the "plat of the city of Zion," the Salt Lake City plan has been named a National Historic Landmark by the American Institute of Certified Planners.

## Crossroads of the West

Often called the "Crossroads of the West," Salt Lake City is the hub of transportation and communication in the Intermountain West. As a modern metropolis, it boasts the prestigious University of Utah with its world-class medical school and faculty, the NBA Utah Jazz basketball team, an arena football team, and the US champion Real Salt Lake soccer team. It has a thriving cultural life with symphony and dance ensembles, and the world-famous Mormon Tabernacle Choir.

In 2002, Salt Lake City hosted the Winter Olympics, introducing the world to its proud religious heritage, friendly hospitality, and Utah's superb roads, magnificent scenery, and year-round outdoor recreation. Salt Lake City is the capital of Utah, which has a population of 2.7 million. While Utah is predominantly Mormon with 68 percent of the population, the city itself is now less than 50 percent Mormon.

Salt Lake City is also the world headquarters for The Church of Jesus Christ of Latter-day Saints. Yet it is not only Mormons who live in Salt Lake City. People from every religion, culture, and ethnic group have been made welcome, as witnessed by the many churches of different denominations.

▲ *"This Is The Place" monument, near the mouth of Emigration Canyon in Salt Lake City, commemorates the courage and determination of the early Mormon pioneers when they arrived in the valley. The monument also honors the Native Americans who lived in the valley, early trappers and explorers, and Catholic friars Dominguez and Escalante, who first traveled through what is now Utah in 1776, keeping detailed journals of their visit.*

▶ *It was the audacious vision of Mormon President Brigham Young that prompted over 60,000 Latter-day Saints to cross the American Great Plains, beginning in the mid-1800s, and establish Salt Lake City as capital of the "Territory of Deseret," now Utah.*

► *Salt Lake City, seen here from the Capitol building looking south, is laid out with wide streets in an orderly pattern. In planning the city's layout, Brigham Young drew on a plat designed by Joseph Smith.*

▼ *While more than half of Utahns are Latter-day Saints, other churches have thrived in the state. The Mormon Tabernacle Choir and Orchestra at Temple Square, shown here, perform at the Cathedral of the Madeleine, a celebrated Roman Catholic church in Salt Lake City.*

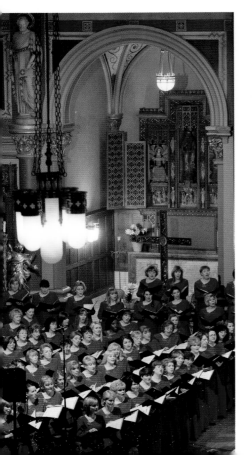

## Utah

Utah is mostly mountainous, with a string of valleys north and south of Salt Lake City. Only four percent of its terrain is suitable for crops. Once based mainly on agriculture, Utah's economy now includes tourism, agriculture, mining, information technology, finance, and oil production. In 1896, when the State of Utah was admitted into the Union, the Federal Government carved the vast territory of Deseret which Brigham Young had colonized into several states.

Widely appreciated as a first-rate vacation destination, Utah is well known for its gorgeous scenery. In summer, its breathtaking mountain valleys and canyons draw backwoods hikers and trail bikers. In winter, Utah's famous snow attracts skiers and snowboarders. From Bear Lake in the north to Zion National Park in the south, visitors fall in love with this rugged frontier, whose many amenities offers them a break from everyday life, whether they are seeking relaxation or adventure.

▲▲ *Bridal Veil Falls in Provo Canyon above the Provo River, one of America's premier trout fisheries.*

▲ *The sun sets over Utah Lake in the central part of the state.*

▶ *These rock formations at Bryce Canyon National Park highlight some of the beauties that can be explored in Utah.*

◀ *Park City, shown here, was the site for ski venues during the 2002 Winter Olympic Games. Skiers come from across the world to enjoy Utah's famous snow, visiting resorts statewide.*

# 3

# Joseph Smith and the Restoration

**Susan Easton Black**

THE RESTORATION OF CHRIST'S CHURCH IN THE MODERN era began with a young boy's search for religious truth. The boy's name was Joseph Smith, the year was 1820, and the place Palmyra, New York. Joseph was anxious to know which church to join because of the religious confusion in his neighborhood caused by the revivalism sweeping the area. As he read in the Bible, "If any of you lack wisdom, let him ask of God" (James 1:5), Joseph came to the conclusion that he should pray to the Lord for guidance.

Retiring to the woods near his family home, he poured out his soul to God. In answer, he had a vision in which a pillar of light brighter than the sun came down and fell upon him. "I saw two Personages," he wrote, "whose brightness and glory defy all description, standing above me in the air. One of them spake unto me, calling me by name and said, pointing to the other—This is My Beloved Son. Hear Him!" (JS–H 1:15–17). Joseph was told not to join any of the churches, but that if he was faithful, the fullness of the gospel—which was not on the earth at that time—would be made known to him.[1]

When Joseph told others of his vision, he was persecuted. Clergy and a violent group in Palmyra turned people against him. The idea that God had spoken to a young boy in modern times challenged their religious beliefs. As Palmyra resident Thomas Taylor explained, "There was something about him they could not understand; some way he knew more than they did, and it made them mad."[2] Yet Joseph would not deny having seen the vision: "Though I was hated and persecuted for saying that I had seen a vision, yet it was true. . . . I knew it, and I knew that God knew it, and I could not deny it" (JS–H 1:22, 25).

## The Book of Mormon

Three years after Joseph's vision, on September 21, 1823, as he again sought the Lord in prayer, a "personage appeared at [his] bedside, standing in the air, for his feet did not touch the floor" (JS–H 1:30). The angelic personage, named Moroni, told Joseph that God had a work for him to do (JS–H 1:33). The work was to translate ancient records, which contained the history of the former inhabitants of the Americas and "the fulness of the everlasting Gospel," as delivered to them "by the Savior" (JS–H 1:34). These records, written on gold plates, had been buried in a hill near his home. When Joseph went to the hill, he found the plates in a stone box under a large stone (JS–H 1:51). Joseph attempted to remove them from the box, but was prevented by the angel, who told him that "the time for bringing them forth had not yet arrived, neither would it, until four years from that time" (JS–H 1:53). During the interim, Joseph married Emma Hale of Harmony, Pennsylvania.

On September 22, 1827, Joseph received the plates containing the ancient record from the angel Moroni "with this charge: that I should be responsible for them; that if I

should let them go carelessly, or through any neglect of mine, I should be cut off" (JS–H 1:59). Joseph protected the plates by hiding them in various places around the family farm, but they soon attracted the attention of thieves. Joseph and Emma, as a result, moved to the home of Emma's father, Isaac Hale, in Harmony, Pennsylvania, where they lived until they acquired a home of their own nearby.

Within the Smith home, translation of the ancient plates from an unknown ancient language began under divine inspiration. Emma, who acted as one of the scribes, was impressed that Joseph dictated for hours without revising the text at all, and after long breaks would continue exactly where he had left off[3] (see sidebar, page 53). Several others besides Emma acted as scribes for Joseph during the translation process, the principal scribe being a schoolteacher, Oliver Cowdery.

◄ *In September 1823, an angel identifying himself as Moroni appeared to Joseph, telling him that God had a work for him to do that would involve the translation of an ancient record.*

◄◄ *When Joseph told others about his vision in the grove, he was ridiculed, but he refused to deny the experience. "I had seen a vision; I knew it, and I knew that God knew it, and I could not deny it," he later wrote (JS—H 1:25).*

► *Mormons believe Peter, James, and John appeared to Joseph and Oliver Cowdery in 1829, restoring priesthood authority that had been taken from the earth after the death of Christ and the Apostles.*

▼ *Joseph married Emma Hale of Harmony, Pennsylvania, in 1827. Soon after their marriage, Emma served as one of Joseph's scribes as he translated the Book of Mormon.*

## Priesthood Authority and Establishment of the Church

In spring 1829, Joseph and Oliver desired baptism, but lacked the priesthood or divine authority necessary to perform such a sacred ordinance. On May 15, 1829, after praying to the Lord near the bank of the Susquehanna River, John the Baptist appeared as a resurrected being, and, laying his hands on their heads, gave them the Aaronic Priesthood—the authority to perform outward ordinances. They then baptized each other (JS—H 68–71).

A few weeks later, Joseph and Oliver received the keys of the Melchizedek Priesthood from the Apostles Peter, James, and John. In this way, the divine authority held by Christ's Apostles was brought back to the earth. In the Bible, this authority is referred to as being "after the order of Melchisedec" (see Heb. 7:17, Matt. 10:1). Its restoration in the 19th century opened the way for the restoration of the Church of Jesus Christ as it had existed in ancient times.

When the translation was nearing completion, three men—Oliver Cowdery, David Whitmer, and Martin Harris— were privileged to be shown the ancient plates by the angel Moroni. They wrote: "We, through the grace of God the Father, and our Lord Jesus Christ, have seen the plates which contain this record. . . . And we also know that they have been translated by the gift and power of God, for his voice hath declared it

▲ *Oliver Cowdery (left), David Whitmer (center), and Martin Harris (right) were shown the ancient plates by an angel, and testified of their experience.*

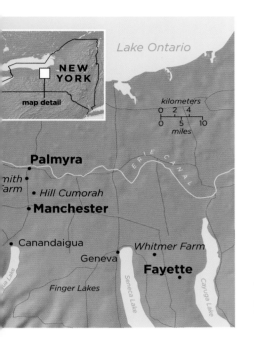

unto us; wherefore we know of a surety that the work is true." Joseph Smith showed the plates to eight others—and they also testified to having seen the plates—before the Book of Mormon was published in March 1830.

Believers in the truth of the Book of Mormon looked forward to the fulfillment of the Lord's promise that "if this generation harden not their hearts, I will establish my church among them" (D&C 10:53). About fifty such believers, referred to as Saints, met in the home of Peter Whitmer, Sr., in Fayette, New York, on April 6, 1830, and the new Church was organized with six charter members. This was the first meeting of what would become The Church of Jesus Christ of Latter-day Saints. (The term "Mormonism," used popularly to describe the religion, is a nickname, which comes from belief in the Book of Mormon.) At that meeting, Joseph Smith was recognized as "a seer, a translator, a prophet, an apostle of Jesus Christ, an elder of the church through the will of God the Father, and the grace of your Lord Jesus Christ" (D&C 21:1).

As word of the Church spread, many opened their houses to the Saints. "Our meetings were well attended," wrote Joseph, "and many began to pray fervently to Almighty God, that He would give them wisdom to understand the truth."[4] In western New York, young and old, both the learned and the illiterate, listened to and embraced the teachings of the "restored" gospel as taught to them by Joseph Smith and early missionaries.

▲ *Map showing the area surrounding Joseph Smith's home in Palmyra, New York, where much of the early history of the Church occurred.*

▶ *The Peter Whitmer, Sr., home (restored) in Fayette, New York, was where Joseph Smith officially organized The Church of Jesus Christ of Latter-day Saints on April 6, 1830.*

◀ *Portraits of Joseph Smith. The painting in the upper right was completed during Joseph's lifetime, while the others are modern interpretations.*

## Relocation to Ohio and Missouri

But soon members of the new faith were being persecuted. In February 1831, in response to the Lord's command to gather in Ohio, Joseph and hundreds of Saints moved from western New York to Kirtland, Ohio. This alarmed an editor of the *Painesville Telegraph*, who wrote that "about two hundred men, women and children, of the deluded followers of Jo Smith's Bible speculation," had arrived. "If the growth of the Church were not soon halted, inhabitants of Kirtland would be governed by the revelations of the Mormon Prophet,"[5] he warned. His fears seemed justified, for the Saints turned Kirtland into a mushrooming community that was larger and, some said, more notable than the Ohio towns of Chardon, Painesville, Akron, Canton, Warren, and Youngstown. Joseph Smith orchestrated this growth.

He also orchestrated similar growth in Jackson County, Missouri, in which he established another settlement in 1831. In Jackson County, Joseph's followers were invited to live the law of consecration and stewardship and create a Zion-like community known as "New Jerusalem." In that community, they were to build a temple, or house of the Lord, in which to worship Jesus Christ.

When they attempted to fulfill these invitations, persecution raged, and the Saints were eventually expelled from the county. Joseph explained why: On the Missouri frontier, the Saints "were settling among a ferocious set of mobbers, like lambs among wolves."[6] The Missourians in Jackson found Mormonism a strange and threatening religion and ridiculed and intimidated adherents of the faith.

Disturbed by the unrelenting harassment upon his friends, Joseph counseled them to rise above retaliation and resolve to build New Jerusalem despite outward challenges.

Encouraged by his words, his followers clutched hammers, shovels, and spades, determined to build the prophesied community. But their dreams were thwarted by angry mobs. Forced to relocate from county to county, the Saints eventually settled in 1837 in Far West, Missouri, and surrounding areas.

### Building the Kirtland Temple

With more than one community underway, additional revelations from God now instructed Joseph to call officers—apostles, seventies, bishops, and other leaders—to help administer the affairs of the Church's increasing membership. He was also instructed to build a temple in Kirtland, a "house of prayer, a house of fasting, a house of faith, a house of learning, a house of glory, a house of order, a house of God" (D&C 88:119).

Even though the Church was so poor that "there was not a scraper and hardly a plow that could be found among the Saints," they eagerly began construction.[7] A rowdy mob tried to stop work on the temple, but the Saints spared no effort in their determination to protect and finish the Lord's house.[8] It was dedicated on March 27, 1836. A week later, Jesus Christ appeared to Joseph Smith and Oliver Cowdery to declare His acceptance of the house. As well, the ancient prophets Moses, Elias, and Elijah appeared to restore the priesthood "keys" (or powers) they held, for the furtherance of the Lord's work in the modern era. It was a time of great rejoicing.

Unfortunately, soon after these spiritual manifestations, the closely knit Mormon society of Kirtland collapsed. There was an economic recession in the United States in 1837, and this led to the failure of the Kirtland Safety Society Bank, a bank owned and operated by Church leaders. Of this situation, Joseph wrote, "It seemed as though all the powers of earth and hell were combining their influence in an especial manner to overthrow the Church at once, and make a final end."[9] Again the Saints were persecuted. Joseph and his faithful followers "regarded it as unsafe to remain any longer in Kirtland" and made plans to move to Missouri, to gather with members there—not realizing that their troubles in Ohio were only a foreshadowing of what lay ahead.[10]

### Far West, Missouri

Once in Missouri, Joseph advised his followers to rise above any outward challenge and establish new communities in which to worship God. The Saints responded by transforming rolling prairies into enterprising communities, but nothing they did stemmed the growing tide of hatred. Old settlers felt threatened by the Mormon communities and their new doctrines. On October 27, 1838, Missouri Governor Lilburn W. Boggs issued the following order: "The Mormons must be treated as enemies and must be exterminated or driven from the state, if necessary for the public good."[11] Joseph's brother Hyrum tried to find out why the Saints were being attacked and killed. "All we could learn was, that it was because we were 'Mormons.'"[12]

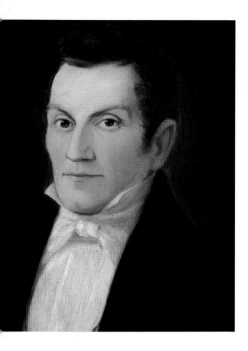

▲ Hyrum Smith, Joseph's older brother, tried to find out why Church members were being expelled from Missouri. "All we could learn was, that it was because we were 'Mormons.'"

◄ The Temple in Kirtland, Ohio, was built by members of the Church during a period of extreme poverty and local opposition. Soon after its dedication, it was the site of remarkable spiritual manifestations. (This historic building is owned by the Community of Christ.)

In the fall of 1838, near the Mormon community of Far West, Missouri, where the Saints had settled in 1837 after relocating from other counties, Joseph and other Church leaders surrendered to the Missouri militia.[13] They were tried in a military tribunal headed by General Samuel Lucas, who sentenced them to death. General Alexander Doniphan was ordered to carry out their execution. He refused to do so, writing to Lucas: "If you execute these men, I will hold you responsible before an earthly tribunal, so help me God!"[14]

Joseph and his fellow prisoners were not executed. Instead, they were taken to a jail in Independence, Missouri, and from there to a jail in Richmond, Missouri. Of his imprisonment in Richmond, Joseph wrote: "We are prisoners in chains, and under strong guards, for Christ['s] sake and for no other cause. . . . We are in good spirits and rejoice that we are counted worthy to be persecuted for Christ['s] sake."[15]

The court system in Richmond, dominated by "the spirit of persecution and malice," failed to protect them.[16] On December 1, 1838, Joseph and five other Latter-day Saint prisoners were moved to the jail in Liberty, Missouri. The unofficial reason given for their continuing imprisonment was that "there was no law for the Mormons in the State of Missouri."[17]

The imprisonment in Liberty Jail—without heat in the cold of winter—lasted more than four months. While imprisoned, Joseph appealed to the Lord, "O God, where art thou? And where is the pavilion that covereth thy hiding place? How long shall thy hand be stayed, and thine eye, yea thy pure eye, behold from the eternal heavens the wrongs of thy people and of thy servants, and thine ear be penetrated with their cries?" (D&C 121:1–2). The Lord answered, "My son, peace be unto thy soul; thine adversity and thine afflictions shall be but a small moment; And then, if thou endure it well, God shall exalt thee on high; thou shalt triumph over all thy foes" (D&C 121:7–8).

In early April 1839, the Mormon prisoners escaped as they were being moved to another jail. They journeyed to Quincy, Illinois, where they were welcomed by the Saints who had previously fled from Missouri. It was not long before Joseph and his followers moved on to Commerce, Illinois, where they had been advised to build another city. Under Joseph's direction, craftsmen, artisans, and skilled laborers tamed a swamp, reclaimed a wilderness, and built the progressive community called Nauvoo—with an eventual population of more than 11,000.[18]

In Nauvoo, under Joseph's direction, the Saints again began to build a temple, more magnificent than that built in Kirtland. But, once again persecutions arose. Jealous of the emerging city's prosperity, leaders of neighboring

◄ *For four months during the winter of 1838–39, Joseph Smith and five others were imprisoned in a primitive jail at Liberty, Missouri, without charges.*

► *This monument was erected on the site of the jail in Carthage, Illinois, where Joseph and Hyrum Smith were killed in 1844.*

▼ *In 1838, General Alexander Doniphan of the Missouri militia refused to carry out the execution of Joseph Smith and other Church leaders when ordered to do so, writing to his commanding officer, "If you execute these men, I will hold you responsible before an earthly tribunal, so help me God!"*

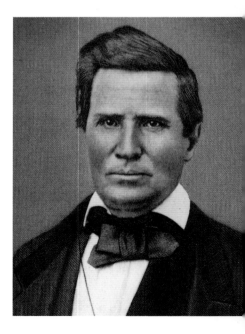

communities threatened violence if the Saints did not abandon their holdings and leave Illinois. Joseph refused to leave. He declared, "I am ready to be offered a sacrifice for this people; for what can our enemies do? Only kill the body, and their power is then at an end."[19]

Joseph's calm resolve was tested in June 1844 when an anti-Mormon newspaper, the *Nauvoo Expositor,* called for the repeal of the Nauvoo City Charter, which officially recognized the lawful existence of the city of Nauvoo. An order issued by the Nauvoo City Council demanding that the *Expositor* immediately cease printing led to the arrest of Joseph and Hyrum. Although the Smith brothers were discharged twice, the legal process did not pacify their enemies. The brothers tried to escape a martyr's fate by crossing the Mississippi into Iowa Territory, but were thwarted as a result of unwise friends advising them to submit to the law administered in Carthage, Illinois.

On June 25, 1844, Joseph and Hyrum were imprisoned in Carthage Jail. Two days later, on June 27, "an armed mob—painted black—of from 150 to 200 persons" surrounded the jail (D&C 135:1). Hyrum was the first to fall from an assassin's bullet. Within moments, Joseph was also shot to death. His last words were *"O Lord, my God!"* (D&C 135:1).

In announcing the death of Joseph and Hyrum, an editor of the *New York Herald* wrote, "The death of the modern mahomet will seal the fate of Mormonism, they cannot get another Joe Smith. . . . The 'latter day saints' have indeed come to the latter day."[20] But such a bold erasure of The Church of Jesus Christ of Latter-day Saints was not to be. Reflecting on the death of Joseph and Hyrum, Elder Orson Hyde predicted that "instead of the work dying, it will be like the mustard stock that was ripe, that a man undertook to throw out of his garden, and scattered seed all over it, and next year it was nothing but mustard. It will be so by shedding the blood of the Prophets—it will make ten saints where there is one now."[21]

## Moving West to the Rocky Mountains

Under the leadership of Brigham Young, the Latter-day Saints continued to gather in Nauvoo and to build a temple there, although mobs threatened them on every side. As the violence increased, many thought of leaving Nauvoo. When some questioned yet another move, Elder John Taylor assured them: "The power that made Nauvoo, that gathered thousands from various climes and kingdoms, that reared the temple, and that whispers to us now, 'peace be still, and see the salvation of God,' can guide us to bring forth a better city, an hundred fold of gathering, and five times as good a temple."[22]

The Saints, under the guidance of Brigham Young, decided to vacate Nauvoo and move west beyond the reach of their persecutors. The first Latter-day Saint to leave Nauvoo was Charles Shumway. On February 4, 1846, in nearly zero-degree weather, Shumway loaded his ox-drawn wagon onto a flatboat, crossed the Mississippi River, and began the first leg of the famed Mormon trek to the Rocky Mountains. Other Saints crossed the river to join Shumway that first day. On flatboats, old lighters, and skiffs, the Saints formed a makeshift fleet to carry the exiles from Illinois to Iowa across the river. From there, they struggled 350 miles west, to Winter Quarters (near present-day Omaha, Nebraska), where they wintered along the banks of the Missouri River in 1846–47.

The wintry conditions faced in Iowa and Nebraska were deplorable, but the Saints pressed on. Artisans, shop-keepers, and farmers became Mormon pioneers seeking refuge from persecution and hatred. Their sacrifice and suffering from the hills of Iowa to the barren plains of Nebraska marked a historic migration of magnificent proportions.

*▲ The Mormon Trail is a 1,300-mile route from Nauvoo, Illinois, to Salt Lake City, used by Mormon pioneers from 1846 until 1869, when the first transcontinental railroad was completed.*

*◄ The Latter-day Saints began vacating their homes in Nauvoo, Illinois, in 1846, hoping to find a place in the west where they could live free from persecution.*

*▼ Brigham Young succeeded Joseph Smith as leader of the Church after Joseph's death in 1844. He was sustained as the prophet and President of The Church of Jesus Christ of Latter-day Saints in 1847 during the exodus west.*

In spring of 1847, the first company of Mormon pioneers, under the leadership of Brigham Young, trekked nearly 1,000 miles west to settle in the Rockies. "This is the right place, drive on," Brigham Young said on July 24, 1847, as he looked over the semiarid desert of the Great Salt Lake Valley.[23] These words were echoed in correspondence to Charles C. Rich: "Let all the brethren and Sisters cheer up their hearts, and know assuredly that God has heard and answered their prayers and ours, and led us to a goodly land."[24]

Intending to guide additional Saints to their new home, Brigham Young returned to the bluffs of the Missouri River. There, near Winter Quarters, in Kanesville, Iowa, he was sustained in December 1847 as prophet and President of The Church of Jesus Christ of Latter-day Saints, fulfilling the prophesy given by Joseph Smith many years before in Kirtland: "The time will come when Brigham Young will preside over this church."[25]

Brigham Young served faithfully for 30 years. His contributions to the Church and kingdom of God are immeasurable. As President he faced multiple problems of emigration, settling, and religious persecution. Yet he never swerved in his conviction to the faith. "We have been kicked out of the frying-pan into the fire," he said, "out of the fire into the middle of the floor, and here we are and here we will stay." He knew that God had revealed to him "that this is the spot to locate His people, and here is where we will prosper."[26]

In crossing the plains, many of the Latter-day Saints lost their lives, but few lost their faith. More than 60,000 Mormon pioneers—3,000 pulling handcarts—crossed the plains until 1869, when the continental railroad came. The Mormon pioneers faced many perils on the trek, but their spirits were not dampened. They later went on to found hundreds of settlements in the Intermountain West. In so doing, they left a legacy of courage and rugged determination in the annals of American history.

---

## Notes

1   Joseph Smith, *History of the Church of Jesus Christ of Latter-day Saints,* 7 vols. (Salt Lake City: Deseret Book, 1976-80 [C 1932-51]), 4:583.
2   *Juvenile Instructor,* October 1, 1882, 302.
3   "Last Testimony of Sister Emma," *The Saints' Herald,* 26 (October 1, 1879), 290.
4   Smith, *History of the Church,* 1:81.
5   *Painesville Telegraph,* April 17, 1835, May 17, 1831.
6   Smith, *History of the Church,* 1:269.
7   Ibid., 1:349.
8   Lucy Mack Smith, *History of Joseph Smith by His Mother* (Salt Lake City: Bookcraft, 1956), 231.
9   Smith, *History of the Church,* 2: 487.
10  Lucy Mack Smith, *History of Joseph Smith,* 247.
11  Correspondence from Governor Lilburn W. Boggs to Headquarters Militia, City of Jefferson, October 27, 1838, as cited in Smith, *History of the Church,* 3:175.
12  Smith, *History of the Church,* 3:420, 3:67.
13  Parley P. Pratt, *Autobiography of Parley P. Pratt* (Salt Lake City: Deseret Book, 1985), 186.
14  Smith, *History of the Church,* 3:190–91.
15  Joseph Smith to Emma Smith, November 12, 1838, as cited in Dean C. Jessee., ed. *The Personal Writings of Joseph Smith* (Salt Lake City: Deseret Book, 1984), 368.
16  Ibid.
17  Pratt, *Autobiography of Parley P. Pratt,* 219–20, 222.
18  George A. Smith, "Historical Address by President George A. Smith," Brigham Young *Journal of Discourses,* 26 vols., (London: Latter-day Saints' Book Depot, 1854-86), 13:115.
19  Smith, *History of the Church,* 6:500.
20  *New York Herald,* July 8, 1844.
21  Smith, *History of the Church,* 7:198.
22  "To Our Patrons," *Nauvoo Neighbor* 3, no. 23 (October 29, 1845), 2 (col. 6).
23  B. H. Roberts, *A Comprehensive History of the Church of Jesus Christ of Latter-day Saints, Century I,* 6 vols. (Salt Lake City: Deseret News Press, 1930), 3:224.
24  Letter of Brigham Young to Charles C. Rich, August 2, 1847, as cited in Leonard J. Arrington, *Charles C. Rich, Mormon General and Western Frontiersman* (Provo, Utah: Brigham Young University Press, 1974), 118.
25  Roberts, *Comprehensive History,* 1:289.
26  James S. Brown, *Life of a Pioneer* (Salt Lake City: George Q. Cannon & Sons, 1900), 121–22.

◄ To Them of the Last Wagon.
*The covered wagon pulled by either horses or oxen was the mainstay for crossing the plains. Those in the last wagon of the pioneer company depicted here were frequently suffering from illness or had other difficulties. Hans Ulrich Bryner, a blind Swiss convert, walked nearly 1,000 miles to Utah behind a wagon such as this. His grandson Lynn Fausett painted this panoramic view.*

# Jesus Christ and the Plan of Salvation

**Brent L. Top**

◀ *Jesus teaches the rich young ruler about discipleship (Luke 18:18–25). The Savior's teachings continue to be the doctrinal foundation of the Church.*

▼ *In the Sermon on the Mount, Jesus said, "Consider the lilies of the field, how they grow; they toil not, neither do they spin: And yet I say unto you, That even Solomon in all his glory was not arrayed like one of these" (Matt. 6:28-29). He taught that God would provide for His children, even as He provides for his other creations.*

JOSEPH SMITH, FOUNDER AND FIRST PROPHET OF THE Church of Jesus Christ of Latter-day Saints, declared: "The fundamental principles of our religion are the testimony of the Apostles and Prophets concerning Jesus Christ, that He died, was buried, and rose again the third day, and ascended into heaven; and all other things which pertain to our religion are only appendages to it."[1] Jesus Christ is the center of Latter-day Saint worship. Like other Christians, Latter-day Saints believe that Christ was literally the Son of God. All that is taught and practiced within the Church has meaning and efficacy only because of the Savior and His infinite Atonement for all mankind.

For Mormons, the term "Atonement" refers to Jesus Christ's suffering in Gethsemane and His death on the cross. He suffered the full weight of the pain and anguish of the sins of all mankind—thus satisfying the eternal law of justice—so that those who repent and accept Christ as their Savior will not have to experience the same punishment (D&C 19:16). Because He personally went through all the pain man is capable of experiencing, He knows how to judge, comfort, and heal each one of us (D&C 88:6, Alma 7:12). Latter-day Saints believe that only through Christ's intercession can fallen man

be reconciled to Heavenly Father. In other words, no amount of human effort can on its own cleanse men from sin or rescue them from death; mankind can fully partake of the blessings of Jesus Christ's Atonement only through the principles and ordinances of His gospel.

## The Plan of Salvation

Latter-day Saints believe, as the Apostle Paul taught, that all mankind is "the offspring of God" (Acts 17:22–29) and that *we lived with Him* before being born on earth. God is a personal Being who loves His children and wants to guide them back to His presence. God's greatest happiness—in fact, His "work and glory"—is "to bring to pass the immortality and eternal life of man" (Moses 1:39). Jesus Christ was chosen as the Savior of mankind in this divine plan, which Mormons call the "plan of happiness" or the "plan of salvation."

In our "pre-existence"—our pre-mortal life—we did not have earthly bodies of flesh and bone, but were spirits. It was a period of preparation— a realm where the spirit sons and daughters of God received "their first lessons" (D&C 138:56) and rejoiced at the prospect of an earthly life away from God's presence in which they would be tested to see if they would "do all things whatever the Lord their God shall command them" (Job 38:7, Abr. 3:25). This "probation" period on earth would be for their personal growth and development.

We cannot remember our time as spirits in the presence of God because a "veil of forgetfulness" was placed over our minds, making it necessary to live by faith here on earth. To help us in our mortal journey, Heavenly Father gave us a special gift, namely our conscience, our "moral compass." Latter-day Saints call this gift the "light of Christ," which "is given to every man, that he may know good from evil" and be motivated "to do good" (Moro. 7:16).

Thus, in His "plan of salvation," Heavenly Father created the earth as a place for His children to obtain physical bodies, develop faith, be tested, and gain the necessary experiences to help them become like Him. Central to God's plan for His children is the Atonement of Jesus Christ, the Son of God.

### First Principles and Ordinances of the Gospel

Faith in the Lord Jesus Christ is the first principle of the gospel. Latter-day Saints believe that faith is manifest in how we love, serve, and worship Jesus Christ, and that salvation is not "earned" by good works alone; it truly is God's gift to those who accept His Only Begotten Son (John 3:16). Latter-day Saints seek to follow Jesus' admonition to His disciples, "If ye love me, keep my commandments" (John 14:15).

The next principle of the gospel is repentance. Acceptance of Jesus Christ as one's personal Savior is essentially linked to repentance—seeking forgiveness for sins, praying for the strength to resist temptation and make necessary changes, and living in harmony with God's will.

Faith and repentance prepare men and women to make covenants. A covenant is a binding solemn agreement between God and man in which man promises to obey God, and God promises to give blessings both here and hereafter. Covenants are often made by means of sacred ordinances, known in some religious traditions as "sacraments." To Latter-day Saints, ordinances administered by those with proper authority are essential components in God's plan of salvation. As Jesus taught Nicodemus about the ordinance of baptism, "Except a man be born of water and of the Spirit, he cannot enter into the kingdom of God" (John 3:5).

Because baptism is a covenant to follow Jesus Christ willingly, Latter-day Saints believe that one must have sufficient understanding of the gospel before choosing to be baptized. They do not baptize infants, believing that little children and others who are not capable of understanding God's commandments, are "alive in Christ" through His grace

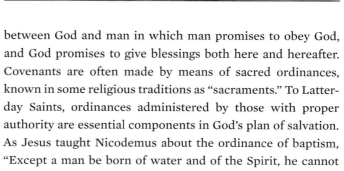

◄ *Latter-day Saints baptize by immersion for the remission of sins. Only those who are accountable for their choices and actions, have faith in Christ and His gospel, and are desirous to covenant with God to serve Him and keep His commandments, are admitted into the Church by baptism.*

▲ *After baptism, a person receives confirmation by the laying on of hands and is given the gift of the Holy Ghost—the promise of additional spiritual guidance and comfort through the influence of the Holy Spirit.*

▶ *Jesus was baptized by John the Baptist to "fulfil all righteousness" (Matt. 3:15).*

and mercy (Moro. 8:8–17). The minimum age for Latter-day Saint baptism is eight years old.

Baptism by total immersion in water is deeply symbolic to Latter-day Saints. It represents not only Jesus Christ's death, burial, and Resurrection, but also the burying of their old lives of sin and their rebirth to a new life of righteousness and devotion.

Through baptism, Latter-day Saints promise that they will always remember Christ, serve Him, and keep His commandments (Mosiah 18:10). After baptism, Latter-day Saints receive another ordinance—the laying on of hands for the gift of the Holy Ghost. This is performed by one who holds the proper authority, or priesthood. The baptized person is confirmed as a member of The Church of Jesus Christ of

▲ *Priests blessing the sacrament. At LDS worship services, known as sacrament meetings, the emblems of Christ's sacrifice are blessed and passed to the congregation. Latter-day Saints view the partaking of the sacrament as a renewal of one's baptismal covenant and a symbolic reminder of the need to continually look to the Savior for a remission of sins, spiritual sustenance, and ultimate salvation.*

▶ *Deacons—boys ages 12–13 who hold the Aaronic (or lesser) priesthood— pass the sacrament to the congregation during sacrament meeting.*

◀ *Jesus institutes the ordinance of the sacrament at the Last Supper (Matt. 26:26–28)*

Latter-day Saints and given the charge to live in such a way as to be worthy of the companionship of the Holy Spirit.

Each Sunday in their regular worship service, Mormons are reminded of the atoning sacrifice of Christ by sacred hymns, prayers, and sermons. They renew their baptismal covenants by partaking of the sacrament of the Lord's Supper. Jesus instituted this ordinance with His disciples at the Last Supper (Matt. 26: 19–30). The bread and wine—or water, as Latter-day Saints use today—symbolize Christ's body and blood, which were sacrificed during His Atonement for mankind (3 Ne. 18:3–10).

## Following in the Footsteps of Jesus

To Latter-day Saints, religion cannot be merely theoretical. It must also be practical. The faith that a disciple has in his or her mind and heart must be evident in his or her way of life. Disciples must walk a godly walk, not just talk the religious talk. "Pure religion and undefiled before God and the Father is this," the Apostle James taught, "To visit the fatherless and widows in their affliction, and to keep himself unspotted from the world" (James 1:27).

In the Sermon on the Mount, Jesus taught that "every good tree bringeth forth good fruit; but a corrupt tree bringeth forth evil fruit. . . . Wherefore by their fruits ye shall know them" (Matt. 7:17, 20). Mormons believe that true conversion—a living faith in Christ and love for Him, and a meaningful commitment to His gospel—will always produce "good fruits."

Latter-day Saints strive earnestly to love and serve God and their fellow men. They consider the Ten Commandments—including the commandments to keep the Sabbath day holy, and to live honest and virtuous lives—to be as binding now as when they were received on Mount Sinai centuries

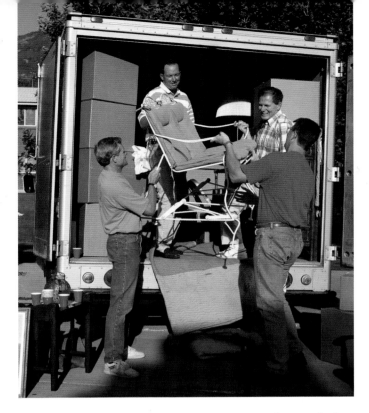

ago. As a measure of their devotion, Mormons observe the law of tithing (see Mal. 3:7–12) and pay 10 percent of their income to the Church for the accomplishment of its purposes (D&C 119:1–7).

Mormons—both individually and collectively—are not perfect, but they desire to be good: good people, good parents, good citizens, good neighbors, good Christians in word and deed. "Let us do good" to all people (Gal. 6:10), taught the Apostle Paul. This is the Christian ideal that Latter-day Saints seek to achieve. "Love is one of the chief characteristics of Deity, and ought to be manifested by those who aspire to be the sons of God," Joseph Smith wrote in 1840. "A man (or woman) filled with the love of God," he observed, "is not content with blessing his family alone, but ranges through the whole world, anxious to bless the whole human race."[2]

## Life after Death

Mormons believe that one's physical body is a house for the spirit that dwells in it. As the author of Ecclesiastes declared, at death "shall the dust return to the earth as it was: and the spirit shall return unto God who gave it" (Eccl. 12:7). In the "spirit world," the place to which our spirits go after this life, those who have been faithful to God will rest from their troubles, while those who have rebelled will be in a state of unhappiness (see Alma 40:12–14). In these conditions, the spirits of all men and women who have died will await the resurrection. Mormons believe that through His Atonement, Jesus Christ broke the bands of physical death, and that all people will live again, taking up their bodies in a literal resurrection, just as Christ did.

A unique tenet of Mormonism teaches that in the period between death and resurrection, people who have died without a knowledge of the plan of salvation will be given the opportunity to learn and accept or reject its principles. In support of this doctrine, Mormons cite the Apostle Peter's testimony that Jesus Christ, in the days between His crucifixion and resurrection, entered the spirit world "and preached unto the spirits in prison" (1 Peter 3:19; 4:6).

At the end of the world, mankind will be "judged out of those things written in the books, according to their works" (Rev. 20:13). Whereas traditional Christianity believes in heaven and hell, Mormons take more literally Christ's declaration that "in my Father's house are many mansions" (John 14:2). Latter-day Saints believe that, as the Apostle Paul taught in 1 Corinthians 15:40–42, there are varying eternal rewards, because of mankind's varying levels of faith, devotion, and desire to be with God.

In 1832, Joseph Smith and his counselor Sidney Rigdon experienced a remarkable vision that revealed three kingdoms

▲ *LDS youth engaged in "Mormon Helping Hands" community service. After a natural disaster, Latter-day Saints, young and old, view service to their fellowmen as an important aspect of their discipleship—a practical, tangible manifestation of their faith in and desire to follow the Master.*

◄ *Members of LDS congregations can be found helping others on a weekly basis. Common service includes helping a neighbor move, as shown here; assisting the elderly with work in the yard or home; taking meals to families that have recently welcomed a new baby; and more.*

► *In the Sermon on the Mount, Jesus taught his followers to do unto others as they would want done unto themselves (Matt. 7:12). This teaching is frequently referred to as the "golden rule."*

▲ *The closing of a casket isn't the closing of existence. Death is not the end. Latter-day Saints believe that life, love, family, and friends extend beyond the death of the mortal body.*

of glory: "celestial," "terrestrial," and "telestial" (D&C 76). These terms parallel those used by the Apostle Paul in his description of resurrected bodies as being in glories as varied as those of the sun, moon, and stars (see 1 Cor. 15:40–42).

All three kingdoms are glorious and are rewards for those who dwell in them. To enter any of the kingdoms requires repentance and acceptance of Jesus Christ. However, the celestial kingdom is reserved for those who sincerely make and keep eternal covenants. Mormons believe that these covenants are the vehicle through which the grace of Jesus Christ is carried into the lives of men and women, changing them into holier beings who are prepared to live with God. According to Latter-day Saint doctrine, the celestial kingdom is the only place where those who have so qualified will live in eternal family units in His divine presence.

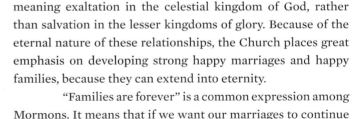

◄ *"He is risen." The resurrected Christ appeared first to Mary Magdalene after his Crucifixion and Resurrection (John 20:11–17).*

▼ *The Mormons' emphasis on families is rooted in the doctrine that marriage is ordained of God and that the family is an eternal unit. Strengthening families is a high priority for the Church.*

## Eternal Families

One of the most important and unique teachings of Mormonism is that marriage and family relationships can continue beyond this mortal life. Marriages of husbands and wives performed in Latter-day Saint temples by those who hold priesthood power are for "time and all eternity," not merely "until death do you part." In Mormon theology, the continuation of the family unit is one of the most important features of "heaven"—meaning exaltation in the celestial kingdom of God, rather than salvation in the lesser kingdoms of glory. Because of the eternal nature of these relationships, the Church places great emphasis on developing strong happy marriages and happy families, because they can extend into eternity.

"Families are forever" is a common expression among Mormons. It means that if we want our marriages to continue beyond death and desire that our families be happy and united forever, then great care and attention must be given to them on earth. David O. McKay, who served as Church President from 1951 to 1970, taught: "I know of no other place than home where more happiness can be found in this life. It is possible to make home a bit of heaven; indeed, I picture heaven to be a continuation of the ideal home."[3]

Understanding the Latter-day Saint view of the eternal plan of salvation gives a deeper and broader perspective to the Mormon emphasis on the family. In September 1995, the Church's governing body, consisting of the First Presidency and the Quorum of the Twelve Apostles, issued an official pronouncement entitled "The Family: A Proclamation to the World." It declares: "The family is ordained of God. Marriage between man and woman is essential to His eternal plan."[4]

The Proclamation stresses that both parents have a responsibility to love and care for each other and for their children, and to bring up their children to be compassionate, law-abiding citizens, observing the commandments of God and following the teachings of the Lord Jesus Christ.

### Notes

1   Joseph Smith, *History of the Church*, 3:30.
2   Ibid, 4:227.
3   David O. McKay, *Gospel Ideals* (Salt Lake City: Bookcraft, 1998), 490.
4   The entire Proclamation may be found at http://mormon.org/family.

# The Bible, the Book of Mormon, and Additional Scriptures

**John W. Welch**

◄ *Carl Heinrich Bloch,* Christ Healing the Sick at Bethesda. *This painting evokes Christ's compassion for all mankind, which sets an example for us to love one another. It also teaches the hopeful message that each of us can be healed both physically and spiritually through Christ.*

▼ *The Book of Mormon: Another Testament of Jesus Christ, is shown here with the other scriptures accepted by the Church. As the subtitle suggests, Mormons view the Book of Mormon as a second witness of the divinity of Jesus Christ. Included in the book is a promise that readers may know of its truth for themselves through humble prayer (Moro. 10:4).*

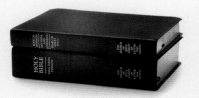

MEMBERS OF THE CHURCH OF JESUS CHRIST OF LATTER-day Saints share with other Christians the firm belief that the Bible is the word of God. They believe that God, in His great love for his children, has revealed His will over the ages to His servants, the prophets, whose writings have become scripture (see Amos 3:7; 2 Pet. 1:20–21). They share the Apostle Paul's view that "all scripture is given by inspiration of God, and is profitable for doctrine, for reproof, for correction, for instruction in righteousness" (2 Tim. 3:16). The scriptures are the texts on which Latter-day Saints base their beliefs and conduct.

What makes Mormons different from most other Christians is their belief that the Bible is not the only scripture. They believe that God has spoken to prophets in many lands and has commanded them to write and declare the words which He speaks to them (2 Ne. 29:11). Latter-day Saints recognize and revere four books of scripture: the Holy Bible, the Book of Mormon, the Doctrine and Covenants, and the Pearl of Great Price. As the standard works of The Church of Jesus Christ of Latter-day Saints, these volumes come together as one great whole.[1]

Both the Bible and the Book of Mormon have been widely misunderstood, if for different reasons. Over the centuries, the Bible has been translated, interpreted, honored, and scorned in numerous ways. The Book of Mormon also has been misunderstood, ignored, or underestimated, as people wonder about its origins and its complementary role as an additional witness that Jesus Christ is the Son of God. As a result of such misunderstandings, the world is the poorer.

Latter-day Saints regret this state of affairs. They would love to see everyone understand the Bible better and are delighted when anyone reads the Book of Mormon. They read both of these sacred books regularly in their personal and family scripture study. When teaching people about the Latter-day Saint faith, the missionaries quote heavily from both the Bible and the Book of Mormon. Both books also play a large part in Mormon talks and religious writings. Two out of every four years, Mormons study the Bible in Sunday School. During the other two years, they cover the Book of Mormon and the Doctrine and Covenants.

Faithful Latter-day Saints love the stories in all these books of scripture: stories about prophets of old who foretold the coming of Jesus Christ, the Son of God; stories about Jesus and His teaching of the gospel; stories of God's covenants with those who faithfully accept Him as their God; and stories about

## The Bible

"The Bible stands at the foundation of The Church of Jesus Christ of Latter-day Saints, constitutes one of its standard works, and is accepted as the word of God."[2] The Bible is foremost among the Church's written guides in faith and doctrine. Latter-day Saints officially use the King James (Authorized) Version of the Bible, which has profoundly shaped modern English language and literature.

The Old Testament offers readers scriptural accounts of the creation and of periods of time when people received commandments from God and made covenants to obey him. Many of these directives, such as the Ten Commandments, remain timeless. Latter-day Saints honor the Abrahamic covenant, through which all people and nations can be blessed, and the Spirit of Elijah, by which all righteous families can be "sealed," or joined together, to live together forever. They honor Moses and Isaiah as two of the greatest prophets of all time. Jesus, in the Old Testament, is foreseen as a future prophet who will be like Moses (Deut. 18:18). Through the keys held by Moses, the Lord's people were gathered and organized.

◄ Head of Christ, *Circle of Rembrandt. Christ's teachings and influence are the preeminent features of all scriptures accepted by Mormons, including the Bible, the Book of Mormon, the Doctrine and Covenants, and the Pearl of Great Price.*

▶ The Prophet Isaiah Foretells Christ's Birth, *by Harry Anderson. The prophet Isaiah wrote of Christ's birth and mission long before those events occurred. The Book of Mormon enriches our understanding of many prophecies concerning Jesus Christ found in the Bible.*

▼ *Christ's Atonement included His suffering in Gethsemane and on the cross, and is a central theme of all Mormon scripture.*

His followers—men, women, and children—who have been taught, blessed, tested, and rewarded for their righteousness.

Latter-day Saints eagerly follow the spiritual teachings and messages in all these books, which tell of God's plan of salvation, His love and His commandments. The scriptures tell Mormons where they have come from, why they are here on this earth, and where they are going as life continues after death.

◄◄ *Joseph Smith was directed by the Angel Moroni to find the golden plates containing the ancient record on the Hill Cumorah near Palmyra, New York.*

▲ *The forested side of the Hill Cumorah as it appears today*

◄ *The Hill Cumorah, Joseph Smith wrote, was "the most elevated of any in the neighborhood. On the west side of this hill, not far from the top, under a stone of considerable size, lay the plates, deposited in a stone box" (JS—H 1:51).*

*▲ Detail of a page of the Original (Dictation) Manuscript of the Book of Mormon, 1829*

## Dictating the Book of Mormon as It Was Translated

The Book of Mormon was dictated by Joseph Smith to scribes, who made a verbatim word-for-word transcription, as seen here, with no punctuation. This page contains the text of 1 Nephi 2:23–3:18. Oliver Cowdery was the scribe for the first 14 lines of this page, but an unidentified scribe began writing mid-sentence on line 15, "I will go and do the things which the Lord hath commanded." This corroborates the testimony of scribes. Joseph's wife, Emma Hale, sometimes his scribe, said that when returning "after meals, or after interruptions, he would at once begin where he had left off, without either seeing the manuscript or having any portion of it read to him. This was a usual thing for him to do. It would have been improbable that a learned man could do this; and, for one so ignorant and unlearned as he was, it was simply impossible." It is noteworthy that very few cross-outs were made throughout this manuscript as the dictation flowed, phrase after phrase.[5]

Isaiah foretold that they would find images of future temples (Isa. 2, 49, 52) and a sealed book that would whisper from the dust of the earth (Isa. 29). In the last days of the world, God would reign on earth (Isa. 10, 13, 52).[3]

In the New Testament, the parts that Latter-day Saints find most important are the accounts of the life of Christ, from His holy birth and baptism to His atoning suffering, death, and Resurrection. They savor His parables, His Sermon on the Mount (Matt. 5–7), His miracles, and His compassion.

They believe that Jesus called and ordained apostles, prophets, elders, deacons, teachers, missionaries, and so forth, while He himself will always be the head of the Church. Their church is organized and authorized in the same way as the New Testament church. Mormons see the New Testament "as the foundation" of the restored gospel of Jesus Christ.[4] Apostles such as Peter, John, and Paul spoke candidly of visitations they had received from the resurrected Lord Jesus, about visions they saw about both the coming hard times, and about the marvelous dispensation of the fullness of times and the final victory of God over the forces of all evil. Latter-day apostles and prophets likewise have had visions and received visitations from the Lord Jesus.

### The Book of Mormon: Another Testament of Jesus Christ

The Book of Mormon is a record left by a group of people, descendants of the Israelite tribe of Joseph, who left Jerusalem approximately 600 years before the birth of Jesus Christ. Led by a prophet named Lehi who was guided by God, they journeyed down the west coast of the Arabian peninsula, built a ship, and sailed to the Americas. The family broke basically into two opposing groups: one fell into disbelief, while the other was favored with a line of inspired prophets and the knowledge of God. The high point of the book is a series of appearances of Jesus Christ following His resurrection as He ministered to these faithful people. The record was compiled and abridged by Mormon and his son Moroni. It ends in AD 421, after the formerly righteous branch of the people had become wicked and were all killed by their enemies. Moroni buried the record with a promise that it would someday come forth to speak "out of the dust" in the name of the Lord (Isa. 29:4).

In the 1820s, Moroni returned to the earth as an angel and told Joseph Smith where the account was buried. Aided by God, Joseph translated the work into English, and it was published in 1830. It has been considered among the most influential books published in 19th-century America, and has since been translated into 107 languages and distributed wherever possible around the world.

Latter-day Saints treasure the Book of Mormon as another testament of Jesus Christ. Repeatedly the Book of Mormon invites all people, everywhere, to believe in the Son of God—that He came to redeem His people, suffered and died to atone for the sins of mankind, and rose from the dead, so that all will be resurrected and will thus stand before God to be judged according to their works. The pages of the Book of Mormon are filled with instructions about believing in Christ, preaching Christ, covenanting with Christ, following Christ, and rejoicing in Christ (2 Ne. 25:26). Those who follow these instructions will come to Christ, avoiding all ungodliness and loving God with all their might, mind, and strength, so that by His grace they will be made perfect in Christ (Moro. 10:32).[6]

Everything in the Bible and Book of Mormon fits together, as can be discerned through the guidance and witness of the Holy Ghost. Both testify of Jesus Christ as the Son of God and Savior of the world. In his final words, Mormon said that the Book of Mormon was "written for the intent that ye may believe [the Bible]; and if ye believe [the Bible] ye will believe this also" (Morm. 7:9). The prophet Ezekiel spoke of two "sticks," that is to say, two scriptural records, or books. Latter-day Saints see the Book of Mormon as one of these sticks—"the stick of Ephraim," written "for Joseph and for all the house of Israel his companions." The other stick is the Bible, the stick of Judah, "written for Judah and for the children of Israel his companions." As Ezekiel prophesied, these two are to be joined "one to another into one stick; and they shall become one in thine hand" (Ezek. 37:16–17).[7]

How can any brief description even begin to scratch the surface of books like these? It takes a lifetime of sympathetic reading and of devoted living to understand what the Bible and the Book of Mormon really say. They are classics that will wear people out long before people will wear them out. The stories of how we got the Bible and the Book of Mormon are truly amazing, even miraculous.[8] But more important than how we got these books is how they inspire us to become more devoted disciples of Jesus Christ.

▶ The Sacrament, *by Minerva Teichert. The Book of Mormon teaches that after Christ's Resurrection, he visited the people of the New World and taught them the same gospel He had taught to the Jews in Galilee and Jerusalem. This painting depicts Christ teaching His disciples to partake of the bread and wine in remembrance of His body and His blood.*

▼ *Print shop of E. B. Grandin (restored). After Joseph Smith translated and dictated the content of the golden plates to scribes, the manuscript pages were taken to this print shop in Palymra, New York, to be typeset, printed, and bound. Copies of the Book of Mormon were available for sale in March, 1830.*

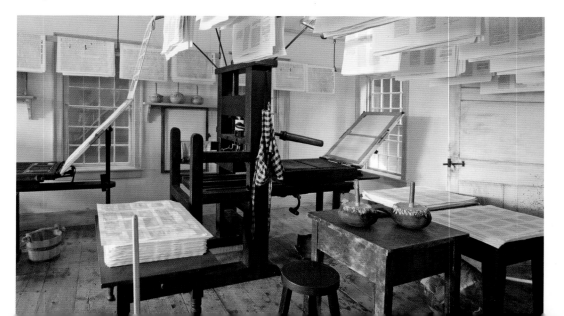

## Additional Scriptures

The ninth Article of Faith set out by Joseph Smith states, "We believe all that God has revealed, all that He does now reveal, and we believe that He will yet reveal many great and important things pertaining to the Kingdom of God." These revelations are found in the Doctrine and Covenants and the Pearl of Great Price.

The Doctrine and Covenants contains 138 sections and two official declarations. Most were received by Joseph Smith for the establishment and governance of the Church. This collection functions as the Church's "open, ever-expanding, ecclesiastical constitution. Its main focus is to build up the Church of Jesus Christ and to bring people into harmony with Christ's kingdom" and "to organize and orient them according to God's mind and kingdom."[9]

The sections of the Doctrine and Covenants come together marvelously. They sound a voice of warning of the coming judgments of God and reveal the plan and way of salvation. They interpret passages in the Bible, organize the offices and quorums of the priesthood, establish Church practices, issue principles and commandments by which all individual members may govern their lives, impart instructions to missionaries proclaiming the gospel of Jesus Christ, give blessings and directions to various individuals, and much more.[10]

The fourth book accepted by Latter-day Saints as scripture is the Pearl of Great Price. The name of this book echoes the parable that Jesus gave about the merchant who went searching for valuable pearls and found "one pearl of great price" (Matt. 13:45–46). It contains the Book of Moses, the Book of Abraham, extracts from Joseph Smith's history (written in 1838), one chapter from his new translation of the Bible (worked on in 1831), and the Articles of Faith (composed in 1842).

The Book of Moses is a grouping of several revelations received by Joseph Smith in 1830 as he sought further knowledge about the calling of Moses as a prophet, the creation of the world, and the otherwise unknown ministry of the prophet Enoch.[11]

The Book of Abraham tells of Abraham's experiences with the Lord in Chaldea, Haran, Canaan, and Egypt. In it Abraham tells of his rescue from official opposition that almost cost him his life, of promises given to him and his descendants, and relates visions he received about the pre-mortal spirits of all human beings, the heavenly council, the periods of creation, and the beginning of human life on this earth.[12]

This part of Joseph Smith's history tells some of the main experiences in his early life, including his search to know which church to join; his vision in 1820 of God the Father and His Son, Jesus Christ; visitations from the resurrected Moroni entrusting to him the task of translating the Book of Mormon into English by the power of God; and the visit of the resurrected John the Baptist giving him and Oliver Cowdery the priesthood power to baptize.[13] His translation of Matthew 24 makes that text clearly more relevant to modern times.

◀ *Smith family home (restored). When 14 years of age, Joseph Smith prayed and received a visitation of God the Father and Jesus Christ in a grove near this home. An excerpt of his history recounting the event is included in the Pearl of Great Price.*

"We believe *all* things, we hope *all* things, we have endured many things, and hope to be able to endure *all* things. If there is *anything* virtuous, lovely, or of good report or praiseworthy, we seek after these things" (A of F 13, italics added).

Many things in the Bible and in all scriptures throughout the world are difficult for mere mortals to understand. Latter-day Saints find that by carefully studying the scriptures, praying for God's enlightenment, and living these teachings, the truth and meaning of sacred things become known. Above all, the scriptures tell us about Jesus (John 5:39). Jesus promised that "if any man will do [God's] will, he shall know of the doctrine, whether it be of God, or whether I speak of myself" (John 7:17). The Bible invites: "If any of you lack wisdom, let him ask of God" (James 1:5); and the Book of Mormon confirms: "By the power of the Holy Ghost ye may know the truth of all things" (Moro. 10:5).

### Notes

1  For the most accessible portal into understanding LDS scriptures, see several hundred entries in the *Encyclopedia of Mormonism,* ed. Daniel H. Ludlow (New York: Macmillan, 1992, cited as *EM*). This valuable reference work is freely available at eom.byu.edu.
2  Victor L. Ludlow, "Bible," *EM,* 1:105; Paul Hedengren, "LDS Belief in the Bible," *EM,* 1:108.
3  See Ellis T. Rasmussen, "Old Testament," *EM,* 3:1027–1030.
4  Robert C. Patch, "New Testament," *EM,* 3:1011.
5  "Last Testimony of Sister Emma," *Saints' Herald* 26 (October 1, 1879): 289–90; John W. Welch, "The Miraculous Translation of the Book of Mormon" in John W. Welch, ed., *Opening the Heavens: Accounts of Divine Manifestations,* 1820–1844 (Provo: Brigham Young University Press, 2005), 76–213, quote on 131.
6  See Monte S. Nyman and Lisa Bolin Hawkins, "Book of Mormon: Overview," *EM,* 1:139–43, followed by dozens of articles about the various books, personalities, and topical interests in the Book of Mormon.
7  Keith H. Meservy, "Book of Mormon, Biblical Prophecies about," *EM,* 1:158–60.
8  John W. Welch and Tim Rathbone, "Book of Mormon Translation by Joseph Smith," *EM,* 1:210–12.
9  Roy W. Doxey, "Doctrine and Covenants: Overview," *EM,"* 1:405.
10  See C. Max Caldwell, "Doctrine and Covenants: Contents," *EM,* 1:407–09.
11  See Bruce T. Taylor, "Book of Moses," *EM,* 1:216–17.
12  Stephen E. Thompson, "Book of Abraham: Contents," *EM,* 1:135.
13  See Joseph Grant Stevenson, "Joseph Smith–History," and linked articles in *EM,* 2:762–63.
14  David J. Whittaker, "Articles of Faith," *EM,* 1:67.

▲ *Peter Whitmer, Sr., home in Fayette, New York (restored). In this home, Joseph Smith translated a portion of the Book of Mormon and received at least 17 revelations that are included in the Doctrine and Covenants.*

The Pearl of Great Price concludes with the Articles of Faith. These declarations "are not a creed in the traditional Christian sense, but they do provide a useful authoritative summary of fundamental LDS scriptures and beliefs."[14] They also display the abundant ideals and universal breadth of the Latter-day Saint faith: "We believe that through the Atonement of Christ, *all* mankind may be saved" (A of F 3, italics added).

# 6 The Foundation of Apostles and Prophets

**Brent L. Top**

BECAUSE OF GOD'S LOVE FOR ALL HIS CHILDREN, HE HAS provided the means for them to be taught moral and ethical principles while they are on earth, and to be guided and directed in their lives to meet their unique challenges and concerns (Alma 30:8, Moro. 7:15–16). When the gospel of Jesus Christ has been on the earth, the purpose of the Church has been to teach faith in Jesus Christ, to administer the ordinances and covenants of the gospel, and to provide members opportunities to serve their fellow men—necessary steps in coming to know God. This purpose has always been the same, both in ancient times and today.

In every age, God has revealed His will—the great plan of happiness—through His prophets (Amos 3:7). These chosen leaders were given divine authority from the head of the Church, Jesus Christ. When Jesus was on the earth, He ordained twelve Apostles, saying, "Ye have not chosen me, but I have chosen you, and ordained you" (John 15:16). As recorded in Matthew, He gave them power to act in His name and to preach His gospel (Matt. 10:1). This divine authority is called the priesthood. With priesthood power, these chosen leaders were able to administer essential ordinances of salvation to the believers, direct the affairs of Church congregations, and maintain unity in doctrine and practice. Jesus thus established His Church with ordained Apostles and other leaders to preach the gospel and to strengthen the faith of those who had accepted His teachings and covenants.

The Apostle Paul taught that those who accepted the gospel of Jesus Christ—Jew and Gentile—were "fellow-citizens with the saints, and of the household of God" and were "built upon the foundation of the apostles and prophets, Jesus Christ himself being the chief corner stone" (Eph. 2:19–20). Additionally, Paul taught that the Church established by Christ was led and directed by prophets, apostles, evangelists, pastors, and teachers "for the perfecting of the saints, for the work of the ministry, for the edifying of the body of Christ," so that the disciples of Christ would not be "tossed to and fro, and carried about with every wind of doctrine" (Eph. 4:11–14).

Differing from both the Catholic claim of unbroken authority through Peter and the popes and the Protestant claim of "priesthood of all believers," Mormons view their Church as the "restored" (not merely reformed) Church of Jesus Christ. Latter-day Saints believe that with the death of Jesus and the Apostles, the authority to direct the Church and administer the necessary sacraments was lost to the earth. Over the centuries,

conflicts arose concerning Church doctrines and practices. The nature of many Christian teachings, ordinances, and covenants were changed. Creeds and doctrines were adopted that were not based on revelation from God, but were derived from worldly philosophies and political motivations.

Mormons believe that Christ's true Church no longer existed on earth. Though men and women of faith did all they could through the centuries to reform the Church and help bring mankind back to Christ's true principles, reform was not enough. A "restoration"—not merely a reformation—was needed to bring back to the earth the Church with its divine authority from God and Christ's unpolluted principles, covenants, and ordinances. Latter-day Saints believe that this restoration of divine priesthood power was accomplished through the "ministration of angels"— that is to say, that Joseph Smith and his associate Oliver Cowdery received divine authority from angels sent from God, and that the gospel was restored by revelation to a modern prophet, Joseph Smith. Joseph Smith was not a theologian or reformer in the traditional sense of those terms; rather, he was the "Prophet of the Restoration," who was commissioned by God to establish The Church of Jesus Christ of Latter-day Saints, which he did on April 6, 1830.

The claim to have authority from God is the essence of Mormon beliefs regarding the role of the modern Church. As stated in the fifth article of faith, "We believe that a man must be called of God, by prophecy, and by the laying on of hands by those who are in authority, to preach the Gospel and administer in the ordinances thereof." The sixth article of faith affirms: "We believe in the same organization that existed in the Primitive Church, namely, apostles, prophets, pastors, teachers, evangelists, and so forth."

At the organization of the Church in 1830, all of its members could meet together in a log cabin. Today the Church is a worldwide organization with over 14 million members and nearly 30,000 congregations in 150 countries. Though languages and cultures may vary, the doctrines, practices, and purposes of the Church are the same all over the world. The primary purpose of the Church is to help individuals and families come to Christ and partake of the blessings of His gospel. The basic unit of the Church is the home. All that is done in the Church—its programs, organizations, meetings,

▲ *Leaders in the Church serve on a voluntary basis, without pay.*

▼ *The basic unit of the Church is the family—parents and children.*

## What Do Mormons Believe?

*In response to an inquiry from John Wentworth, editor of the* Chicago Democrat, *Joseph Smith penned, in March 1842, thirteen simple and straightforward statements of belief, which have become known as the **Articles of Faith.** Although not a comprehensive treatment of Mormon beliefs and practices, these statements provide a brief summation of some of the most important and distinctive beliefs of the Church.*

1 We believe in God, the Eternal Father, and in His Son, Jesus Christ, and in the Holy Ghost.

2 We believe that men will be punished for their own sins, and not for Adam's transgression.

3 We believe that through the Atonement of Christ, all mankind may be saved, by obedience to the laws and ordinances of the Gospel.

4 We believe that the first principles and ordinances of the Gospel are: first, Faith in the Lord Jesus Christ; second, Repentance; third, Baptism by immersion for the remission of sins; fourth, Laying on of hands for the gift of the Holy Ghost.

5 We believe that a man must be called of God, by prophecy, and by the laying on of hands by those who are in authority, to preach the Gospel and administer in the ordinances thereof.

6 We believe in the same organization that existed in the Primitive Church, namely, apostles, prophets, pastors, teachers, evangelists, and so forth.

7 We believe in the gift of tongues, prophecy, revelation, visions, healing, interpretation of tongues, and so forth.

8 We believe the Bible to be the word of God as far as it is translated correctly;

we also believe the Book of Mormon to be the word of God.

9 We believe all that God has revealed, all that He does now reveal, and we believe that He will yet reveal many great and important things pertaining to the Kingdom of God.

10 We believe in the literal gathering of Israel and in the restoration of the Ten Tribes; that Zion (the New Jerusalem) will be built upon the American continent; that Christ will reign personally upon the earth; and, that the earth will be renewed and receive its paradisiacal glory.

11 We claim the privilege of worshiping Almighty God according to the dictates of our own conscience, and allow all men the same privilege, let them worship how, where, or what they may.

12 We believe in being subject to kings, presidents, rulers, and magistrates, in obeying, honoring, and sustaining the law.

13 We believe in being honest, true, chaste, benevolent, virtuous, and in doing good to all men; indeed, we may say that we follow the admonition of Paul—We believe all things, we hope all things, we have endured many things, and hope to be able to endure all things. If there is anything virtuous, lovely, or of good report or praiseworthy, we seek after these things.

▲ Living Water, *by Simon Dewey. Jesus is teaching the Samaritan woman at Jacob's well (see John 4:5-42). Women are considered equal with men in the Lord's plan.*

and service opportunities—is designed to bless and strengthen individuals and families.

There is no paid professional clergy in The Church of Jesus Christ of Latter-day Saints. Local leaders serve on a voluntary basis and contribute their time, talents, and financial resources for the work of the Church. Although women are not ordained to the priesthood, they serve in partnership with men, providing the primary leadership in organizations for women, teenage girls, and children. Men and women are considered equal in the Lord's plan (2 Ne. 26:33) and receive all the same ordinances and blessings.

Although the leaders receive no pay, such an extensive organization as the Church requires that some men and women be employed to administer its many programs and departments. These include the Church's educational system; translation, printing, and distribution of Church materials; building and maintaining Church facilities; welfare services, and so on. Much of the general administration is done from the headquarters of the Church in Salt Lake City, Utah, though many things are administered and supervised in the various countries where the Church is located.

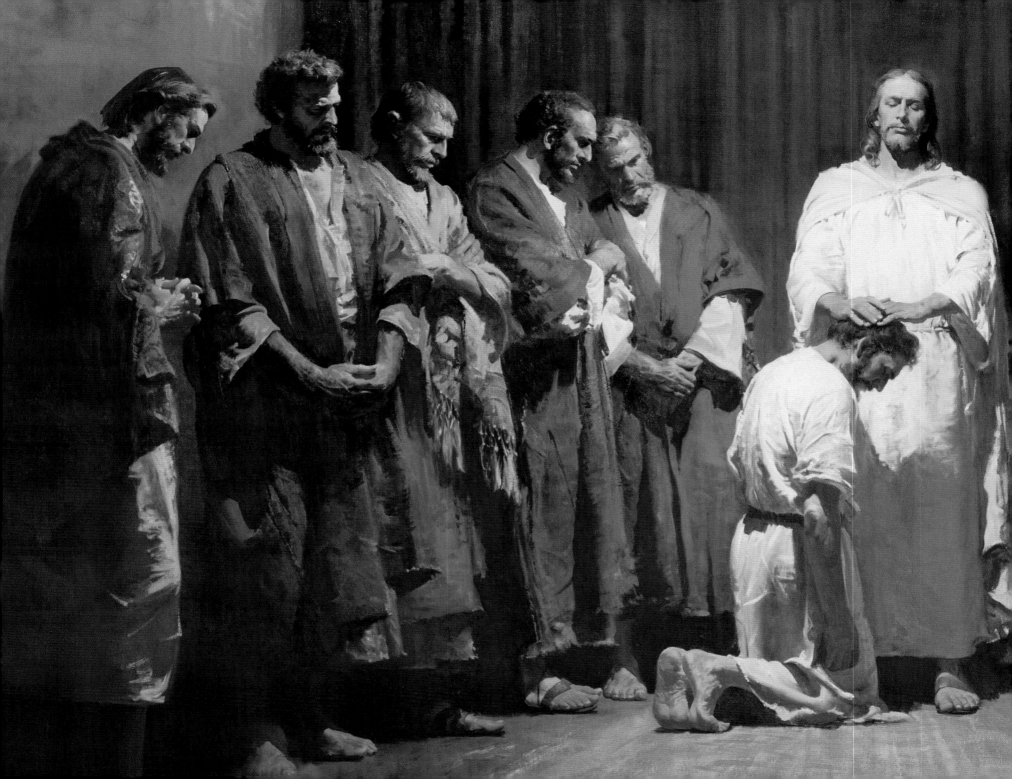

◄ When Christ was upon the earth, he ordained twelve Apostles, and gave them authority to act in His name (see Matt. 10:1). Paul wrote that the Church was "built upon the foundation of the apostles and prophets, Jesus Christ himself being the chief corner stone" (Eph. 2:19–20).

Whether at Church headquarters or in small branches of the Church in remote areas of the world, the fundamental purposes of the Church are: (1) to help the members perfect their lives; (2) to proclaim the gospel throughout the world; (3) to unite generations through family history and temple ordinances; and (4) to care for the poor and needy, both those who are members of the Church and those who are not.

### Living Prophets for a Living Church

"We believe all that God has revealed, all that He does now reveal," states the ninth article of faith, "and we believe that He will yet reveal many great and important things pertaining to the Kingdom of God." Latter-day Saints believe that the heavens are not sealed, that God is still revealing His will to prophets. John Taylor, third President of the Church (1880–87), explained: "We require a living tree—a living fountain—living intelligence, proceeding from the living priesthood in heaven, through the living priesthood on earth. . . . And from the time that Adam first received communication from God . . . it always required new revelations, adapted to the peculiar circumstances in which the churches or individuals were placed. Adam's revelation did not instruct Noah to build his ark; nor did Noah's revelation tell Lot to forsake Sodom; nor did either of these speak of the departure of the children of Israel from Egypt. These all had revelations for themselves. . . . And so must we."[1]

The President of the Church is viewed as the prophet, the earthly head of the Church, and the only person authorized to exercise all the priesthood "keys," or powers to guide the Church. As such, he receives revelation for the whole Church. Latter-day Saints also accept the counselors in the First Presidency and Quorum of the Twelve Apostles—the Church's

chief leaders—as "prophets, seers, and revelators." Mormons believe these men have been called by God and commissioned by Him with priesthood power and authority to declare God's will and direct the affairs of the Church, to testify of Christ, and to expound the doctrines of the gospel. Serving under their direction are other officers of the Church—both those with general authority over the whole Church and those with local jurisdiction—to "preach, teach, expound, exhort," to "watch over the church always," and to teach "according to the covenants" (see D&C 20:38–60; 107:85–100).

In accordance with these scriptural injunctions, the Church convenes a general conference every six months in which prophets and apostles and other officers of the Church teach gospel principles, strengthen faith and spirituality, and give timely counsel to the members of the Church. Although these conferences are convened in the Conference Center in Salt Lake City, Utah, they are broadcast by satellite and via the Internet to congregations and individual homes throughout the world. The proceedings of the meetings are also published in official Church periodicals and posted on official websites.

*▲ Sessions of General Conference are broadcast live from the Conference Center in Salt Lake City twice yearly. Messages from the sessions are also published in the official Church magazines, and are available for reading and viewing on the Church's website at lds.org.*

*▼ More than 20,000 attend each session at the Conference Center near Temple Square in Salt Lake City. Millions more view the sessions via satellite and Internet.*

In addition, these prophets, apostles, and other Church leaders counsel and direct Latter-day Saints at local conferences and leadership training meetings. As in ancient times, prophets and apostles are "special witnesses of the name of Christ in all the world" (D&C 107:23), with a sacred responsibility to travel the world teaching the gospel, ministering to the members, and leading souls to Christ.

Some people are suspicious of a Church that claims to be led by a modern-day prophet "like unto Moses" (see D&C 107:91), assuming that members of such a Church "blindly" obey this prophetic figure. Others think that since the Church places such great emphasis on priesthood authority and leadership hierarchy, it does not allow for individual thought or expression. Such views are misunderstood and do not harmonize with the teachings of the Church.

While Mormons do indeed believe in prophetic revelation, they believe just as strongly in individual choice and accountability and personal revelation. Latter-day Saints are urged to think for themselves, to study and ponder the issues, to personally study the scriptures and the teachings of Church leaders, and to seek for themselves the guidance and direction of the Holy Ghost, within the bounds of their own stewardship and responsibilities. "It is not sufficient for us as Latter-day Saints to follow our leaders and accept their counsel," Harold B. Lee, tenth President of the Church (1972–73) taught, "but we have a greater obligation to gain for ourselves the unshakable testimony of the divine appointment of these men and the witness that what we have told us is the will of our Heavenly Father."[2]

Latter-day Saints seek to follow the teachings of the Master, as found in the scriptures and as expounded by the Lord's servants, with both spiritual conviction and intellectual understanding. As they do so, they are blessed in very practical and also deeply spiritual ways. They take comfort from the assurance that in a troubled world, God continues to guide His children through living prophets, apostles, and inspired local leaders.

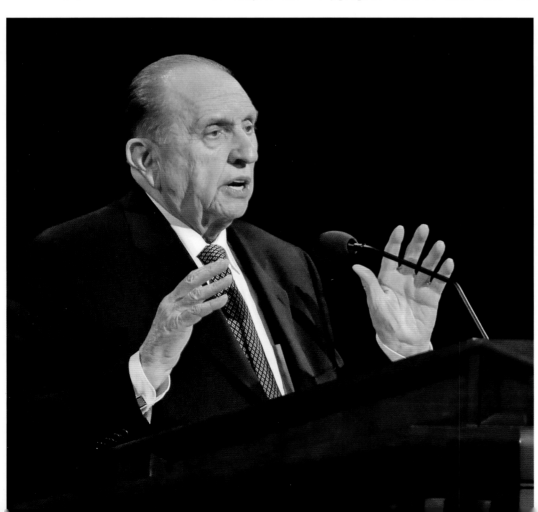

▼ *President Thomas S. Monson speaks at a session of the General Conference. The President of the Church is viewed as the Lord's prophet on the earth.*

### Notes

1  John Taylor, *The Gospel Kingdom,* selected by G. Homer Durham (Salt Lake City: Bookcraft, 1943), 34.
2  Harold B. Lee, in *Official Report of the One Hundred Twenty First Semi-Annual General Conference of The Church of Jesus Christ of Latter-day Saints,* October 1950, 130.

# 7 Meetinghouses and Church Programs

**Brent W. Roberts**

◄ *An LDS meetinghouse stands on a street corner in Harlem, New York.*

▼ *LDS meetinghouses are used for a variety of meetings and activities througout the week. The main Sunday worship service is called sacrament meeting. During this meeting, bread and water that have been blessed by the priesthood are passed to the congregation, in remembrance of the Savior's Atonement.*

IN THE SPRING OF 1844, THE FUTURE MAYOR OF BOSTON, Josiah Quincy, traveled to Nauvoo, Illinois, to visit the founding prophet of The Church of Jesus Christ of Latter-day Saints, Joseph Smith. At the time, the Latter-day Saints, informally called Mormons, were involved in a major building project— constructing a temple to their God, a modern-day "house of the Lord" (Micah 4:1).

Born of privileged pedigree, Quincy was acquainted with grand architecture; nonetheless, he was struck by the Mormons' majestic temple. Calling it a "wonderful structure," and "altogether indescribable,"[1] he couldn't understand why anyone on the American frontier would undertake such a project. For Latter-day Saints, the reason has always been the same. Mormons today build beautiful temples and meeting-houses all around the world in order to teach the gospel of Jesus Christ and help others follow the Savior. They worship Christ in regular Sunday services in their meetinghouses, and invite all to participate with them, as well as in other weekday activities.

## Serving Local Needs

In recent years, the worldwide growth of the Church has necessitated an increasingly expansive building program.

There are over 28,000 congregations of Latter-day Saints throughout the world, and the Church strives to provide adequate facilities for each of these congregations. Former President of the Church Gordon B. Hinckley observed that "we are producing better buildings than have ever previously been constructed in the Church. They combine beauty with great utility. If they look much the same, it is because that is intended. By following tried and tested patterns we save millions of dollars while meeting the needs of our people."[2]

The building program of the Church has developed standard plans, which contain key features to facilitate the worship and activity programs of the Church. In addition, the standard plans establish a uniform look and a way for meetinghouses to be built more efficiently and economically. Of course, the meetinghouses vary in size and design. They are adapted and modified in appearance to the local environment and architectural features of the area. They are designed to fit into the communities in which they are located. Over the years the Church has also taken special pains to make its buildings more environmentally friendly and energy efficient.

When visitors enter a meetinghouse, they will find the layout different than churches or cathedrals of some

◀ *A Latter-day Saint Sunday worship service, called sacrament meeting, is held in the chapel of a meetinghouse in Ghana, Africa.*

▼ *This Latter-day Saint meeting-house is in Phnom Penh, Cambodia.*

▲ *An eight-year-old child is baptized by her father in a meetinghouse font.*

▶ *A recently constructed meeting-house in Provo, Utah. A building like this is usually used by two or three local congregations.*

other Christian denominations. In addition to a chapel, seating from 50 to 300 worshippers, the meetinghouse also includes classrooms, offices, a baptismal font, a kitchen, large assembly areas, and in many cases a cultural hall with an indoor basketball court. These cultural halls are used for a variety of activities, ranging from sports to dramatic or musical productions, from dancing to dining. Often they are positioned in the building to be used as an overflow for larger worship service meetings.

## Spiritual, Social, Athletic, and Cultural Activities

For members of the Church, the meetinghouse is an important hub of their religious life. To them the most important part of the week is the hour-and-ten-minute sacrament meeting, or worship service, which is held in the chapel. The meeting opens with a hymn and a prayer and the sacrament is blessed and passed to the congregation. Men, women, and younger members of the congregation not only pray but give sermons

▲ *The Relief Society is the Church's organization for women.*

based upon the principles of the gospel of Jesus Christ. The sacrament, based on the Last Supper as related in the Bible, consists of bread and water, which is blessed in remembrance of the Savior's Atonement. Members edify and teach each other the principles taught by Jesus Christ. The chapel is considered the most important and sacred room in the meetinghouse.

Additional Sunday meetings focus on strengthening families. Members believe that the family is the fundamental building block of society and that through obedience to the commandments of the Lord Jesus Christ, families can be together forever. Church services are offered to all age groups. Young children are divided by age and taught the most basic but beautiful teachings of the gospel, including making right choices, helping those in need, being honest, loving others as the Savior would, and being a good and faithful friend. Teenagers learn to become responsible adults, good family members, and to honor their parents. Men and women learn how to improve their home life. Classes are offered

on improving marriage relationships and creating a gentle, tranquil spirit in the home. Both men and women learn the importance of leading in their homes through principles of gentleness, kindness, love, charity, and patience.

During weekday evenings, the meetinghouse is used for a variety of purposes. These include activities for the young men and young women 12–18 years old, Boy Scout meetings, Cub Scout pack meetings, leadership training meetings, children activity programs, women's meetings, activities sponsored by local congregations, and wedding receptions.

In some cases, meetinghouses become staging areas for community service initiatives or relief centers during natural disasters. Caring for the poor and needy is an essential element of the gospel of Jesus Christ. On many occasions, these relief efforts are in conjunction with other community organizations and faith-based groups.

## Focus on the Family

For Latter-day Saints, the meetinghouse is very important, but not as important as their own homes. What matters most in their lives is building families and individuals, and their

*◄ Congregational singing is an integral part of the weekly sacrament meeting.*

*▶ Church members and missionaries help pack relief supplies inside a Latter-day Saint meetinghouse in Thailand.*

*▼ Latter-day Saint families meet together in a weekly family home evening, in which they sing, pray, have a short lesson, and enjoy an activity together. Dessert is often the final event of the evening.*

relationship with the Lord Jesus Christ. Harold B. Lee, a former President of the Church, said to parents: "The most important of the Lord's work that you will ever do will be the work you do within the walls of your own home."[3] Members of the Church take very seriously their responsibility to raise and care for their families.

In 1995, the Church issued a proclamation to the world, which stated in part: "Husband and wife have a solemn responsibility to love and care for each other and for their children. 'Children are an heritage of the Lord' (Psalms 127:3). Parents have a sacred duty to rear their children in love and righteousness, to provide for their physical and spiritual needs, to teach them to love and serve one another, to observe the commandments of God and to be law-abiding citizens wherever they live."[4] Members of the Church set aside one evening each week, generally Monday evening, for the spiritual and social nurturing of the family. This is called family home evening.

*◄ Boys participate in the Cub Scout program at their local meetinghouse. The Church was the first institutional sponsor of Scouting in the United States, and currently sponsors more Scouting units than any other organization in the country.*

*► The Young Women's organization in the Church involves classes on Sunday and activity meetings during the week.*

*► Young men play basketball at a Church-sponsored game in the "cultural hall," a large, multi-use room in the meetinghouse.*

### Programs for Every Age Group

Since Church programs are designed to support the institution of the family and strengthen the individual, there are programs for every age group. Women, ages 18 years and older, belong to a worldwide women's organization called the Relief Society. Established in 1842, the Relief Society now boasts six million members, who are organized to teach and inspire women "to build faith and personal righteousness, strengthen families and homes, and help those in need."[5] The Relief Society motto, "Charity Never Faileth," (1 Cor. 13:8), expresses the commitment on behalf of its members to love, nurture, and minister to those in need. Relief Society meetings are held on Sunday as well as during the week. Sunday meetings are devoted to gospel study and improving family relationships, and follow the same course of studies as the men. Weekday meetings may include enrichment classes, service opportunities, and conferences and workshops, designed to teach members provident living and self-reliance, and to increase personal righteousness and faith.

All worthy men, regardless of occupation, education, or training, are ordained to an office in the higher or Melchizedek Priesthood and hold the office of Elder or High Priest. Prospective elders are also included in priesthood classes and service groups as they prepare to receive their ordination. Men who hold the priesthood are organized into service groups, known as quorums, whose main purpose is to teach

the gospel, provide social experience, and give opportunities for service. Part of their training is to become better husbands and fathers. These groups typically meet for a 50-minute instruction period on Sunday while the Relief Society, Young Women, and other groups are meeting, as well as for service and social events during the week. Priesthood quorums provide opportunities for developing leadership skills, as leaders are chosen from their ranks.

Gospel instruction begins at a very young age. Children under the age of 12 meet in Primary each Sunday, where they are taught the principles of the gospel through

lessons, music, and activities that strengthen their individual resolve to be valiant and choose the right. They learn about the scriptures and the power for good that comes from applying

the principles taught in them. Teachings and activities are centered on becoming a better person and family member.

Youth programs are sponsored by the Church for teenagers. Young women ages 12–18 meet together each Sunday and one night every week for lessons and activities designed to strengthen core values, provide sociality, and have fun. These core values include faith, divine nature, individual worth, knowledge, choice and accountability, good works, integrity, and virtue. Young women of the Church believe that as they learn, accept, and act upon these values, they will be prepared to be better family members, mothers, and community members.

Young men of the same age are ordained to offices in the Aaronic or preparatory priesthood. A deacon, aged 12–13, can pass the sacrament; a teacher (an office in the priesthood), aged 14–15, can assist in home visits; and a young man, aged 16–18, ordained a priest, can offer the prayers on the sacrament and has authority to baptize. He, however, does not have

*▲ LDS college students take a break from studies at an LDS Institute of Religion building next to their campus. Other programs for single adults in the Church include Sunday study classes, social activities, and service projects. The Church also has a number of congregations specifically for single adult members.*

*◄ The Church's organization for children ages 3–12 is called Primary, and includes classes and activities that teach the gospel of Jesus Christ using a child-focused curriculum.*

*▶ Mormon young people regularly participate in service projects as a part of their Church-sponsored youth activities.*

authority for the laying on of hands for the gift of the Holy Ghost after baptism, which is reserved for a holder of the higher or Melchizedek priesthood.

Boys are also involved in Boy Scouting activities each week. The Church formally affiliated with Scouting in 1913, the first institutional sponsor of the Scouting movement in the United States, and continues to sponsor more scouting groups than any other organization in the US. The Scouting program encourages young men to be self-reliant, serve others, prepare for emergencies, conserve natural resources, and become actively involved in the community. It also teaches them to be honest, obedient, kind, cheerful, trustworthy, and loyal. Scouting provides opportunities for young men to put into practice the teachings of the Savior Jesus Christ, which they learn in Church and at home.

Children and youth ages 8–18 engage in goal-oriented individual achievement programs, which help them develop skills, abilities and self confidence, and a deeper commitment to living gospel principles.

## Single Adults

Unmarried Church members ages 18–30 have the option of attending Sunday services and social activities together, creating a vibrant spiritual and social haven for those in this unique demographic. Activities are designed to give them a place to call home in today's fast-paced, transient world and offer them opportunities to lead and serve in a familiar setting. Young single adults may be called to help lead entire congregations, teach Sunday school classes, or serve on activity committees, and—along with other members—serve the community by providing volunteer hours or humanitarian aid to those in need. Most young singles in this age group grapple with life's

▲ *This meetinghouse in Bangkok, Thailand, completed in 1972, was the first in that country.*

◄ *The Hyde Park meetinghouse is adjacent to the well-known public space in London, England.*

► *A range of activities is available in the Church for single adults older than 30, including classes, service projects and social events.*

most important and far-reaching decisions, including marriage, education, career, and friendships. A stable yet fun and exciting environment where gospel principles are taught and practiced helps keep life in perspective while planning for the future.

As part of their ministry, Church leaders also provide a wide range of activities tailored to single adults over 30, and Latter-day Saint meetinghouses play an integral role in these activities. Speakers from the Church and the community regularly address groups of single adults on weeknights. Singles attend classes, dances, participate in service projects, and interact socially, but most importantly, they find understanding, strength, and help from each other as they face the difficulties of life.

## Home Visits

The reach of the Church goes beyond the walls of the meeting-house. Church members believe they all have a responsibility to "watch over the church always, and be with and strengthen them" (D&C 20:53). This includes caring for and watching out for their fellow members, lifting them up when they are down, and helping them when they struggle, which in large part is accomplished through home visits. Members, both men and women, are asked to visit assigned members and their families each month. They share spiritual messages, pray with the families, and offer help and assistance. It is commonplace to receive a timely meal if there is sickness in the home, or a gift on a special birthday. Through this program, members are cared for, watched over, and develop a greater desire to serve others.

## Come to Christ

The activities held in meetinghouses—cultural, social, sporting, educational, and sacred—bring members of the Church together. Though these activities are varied, the motivation to build and fill these meetinghouses remains the same. The Church of Jesus Christ of Latter-day Saints strives to help individuals and families come to know their Savior Jesus Christ and become more like Him. Church building and programs are merely vehicles for the accomplishment of these purposes.

### Notes

1   Josiah Quincy, *Figures of the Past* [1883; reprint] (Boston: Little, Brown, 1926), 328.
2   "Condition of the Church," *Ensign*, November 2004, 4.
3   "Strengthening the Home" [Pamphlet, 1973].
4   *Ensign*, November 1995, 102.
5   mormon.org/faq/relief-society/.

# Mormon Lifestyle

**John P. Livingstone**

*◄ Latter-day Saints usually don't appear different from other members of their community.*

*▼ Latter-day Saints believe that scripture study brings them closer to God and reminds them of the covenants they have made to keep His commandments.*

THE LIFESTYLES OF LATTER-DAY SAINTS ARE ACTUALLY much the same as those of others in their community, wherever they live in the world. In other words, Mormons do not necessarily stand out by their dress, speech, or behavior in obvious, public ways. Like their neighbors, they drive cars and go to work each day. They would probably be hard to pick out of a line-up. You would have to look for more subtle nuances to nail down the Mormons in the group on the left.

## Family Focus

Marriage and family are important aspects of Mormonism. Children are taught from a young age that families are eternal and can dwell with God in the next life, and that marriage in a temple is a marriage for eternity. While not all Mormon marriages take place in a temple, and some temple marriages end in divorce, a large percentage of marriages are successful, and many families have a sizable number of children. A 2011 Pew Research Center report states: "Four out of five Mormons (81%) believe that being a good parent is one of the most important goals in life, and roughly three out of four Mormons (73%) put having a successful marriage in this category."[1]

Because of the modesty concerns of their parents, Mormon young women are not as likely to be wearing tank tops or bikinis. The Pew study mentioned above shows that 79% of Latter-day Saints feel that sex between unmarried adults is morally wrong, and this is reflected in their emphasis on modest clothing.[2]

Fidelity in marriage is a cherished goal. "God has commanded that the sacred powers of procreation are to be employed only between man and woman, lawfully wedded as husband and wife."[3] The Church recognizes that some people may have a propensity for same-sex attraction, but the divine laws of sexual conduct apply to all. The Church also warns of the ills of pornography.

Likewise, because of the Church's strong belief in the sanctity of life, abortion is seen as a serious sin, except in the case of rape or other extreme circumstances. The Church is opposed to abortion for personal or social convenience.

## Family Home Evening, Scripture Study, Family Prayer

Since the early years of the 20th century, Church leaders have encouraged families to hold a family night, when parents

▲ *Latter-day Saint families usually have family prayer once or twice a day.*

prays together stays together. When parents teach their little ones to pray early in their lives, children are more likely to follow their parents' example if that example seems sincere. Mormons believe that it is when they act on their beliefs that they are practicing faith. In other words, they feel that talking of faith without action isn't faith.

Family scripture reading is another common practice among Latter-day Saints. Many get up early in the morning to read some scripture and have family prayer before the day's activities get fully underway. Very young children may receive help from parents or older siblings to recite some of the scripture passages until they are old enough to read for themselves.

▲▲ *Scripture study is usually brief but meaningful for family members.*

▲ *Mormons believe that one of their most important goals should be to raise happy families by being good parents.*

◄ *Good food keeps the body healthy and under control of the individual's inner spirit.*

► *Family home evening is observed every Monday, and no other meetings are scheduled regularly on that night.*

spend time with their children and instruct them in the principles of good living. Formally known as family home evening, it is usually held on Monday. Consequently, no other church meetings are scheduled for Monday nights. The family evening may be as unique as the family wishes. Wise parents start early with children and keep their instruction sessions short and interesting, while also having some kind of family activity, and often a treat as well.

In 1995, Church leaders issued a Proclamation on the Family, which laid out definitive guidelines. One line states: "Successful marriages and families are established and maintained on principles of faith, prayer, repentance, forgiveness, respect, love, compassion, work, and wholesome recreational activities."[4]

Another common practice among Mormon families is family prayer. Mormons tend to believe that the family that

## Food and Drink

Since 1833, Latter-day Saints have been encouraged to avoid taking harmful substances into their bodies. The scriptural mandate for this is what is called the "Word of Wisdom," which encourages the use of nutritious food—fresh fruits, vegetables, cereals, and meat sparingly—and prohibits alcohol, tobacco, tea, and coffee. While the Word of Wisdom was not initially prescribed as a binding test of Church membership or fidelity, over the years it has become a test of worthiness: only members abstaining from the above substances and observing other religious rules may participate in temple worship.

Studies have shown that Latter-day Saints tend to live longer—one study suggests as much as six years on average—and escape the mortal diseases associated with tobacco, alcohol, and drug use, as a result of avoiding these harmful substances and eating healthy food.

## Education and Community Service

Most Mormon parents in the United States and many other countries encourage their children to get an education beyond high school. While all do not achieve this, so many earn a college degree that the average educational level of Mormons is above national norms.

Interestingly, the more education Latter-day Saints have, the more they get involved in Church activity, and the more solidly they tend to exercise faith in the Lord.[5] While this tendency runs against the trend in many other religious organizations, Mormons have little trouble rationalizing their beliefs with their education. Mormon scripture says, "The glory of God is intelligence, or, in other words, light and truth"(D&C 93:36); it also says, "Whatever principle of intelligence we attain unto in this life, it will rise with us in the resurrection. And if

a person gains more knowledge and intelligence in this life through his diligence and obedience than another, he will have so much the advantage in the world to come" (D&C 130:18-19).

Because The Church of Jesus Christ of Latter-day Saints is run by lay persons at the local level without a paid ministry, almost everyone has a Church "calling"—an assignment they fill each week. As well as benefiting their local church, this "pitching in" activity often makes Mormons good neighborhood helpers, willing to give assistance as needed in community efforts. Dallin H. Oaks, one of the Church's leaders, commented on this in April 2012 when he said, "All of this is affirmed in a nationwide study which concluded that active members of The Church of Jesus Christ of Latter-day Saints 'volunteer and donate significantly more than the average American and are even more generous in time and money than the upper [20 percent] of religious people in America.' "[6] Latter-day Saints feel that when they are serving their fellow man, they are serving God (Mosiah 2:17).

The missionary program of the Church offers an opportunity for young men aged 18 to 25, and women 19 and up, as well as older couples, to serve as missionaries throughout the world. This missionary service gives Latter-day Saints the opportunity to teach the gospel to people in different parts of the world and different cultures from the one they know. The young men often take their two-year service experience into their marriages and families, where helping out in the community becomes an extension of their selfless service learned through their missionary experience.

## Mormons in Politics

Mormons often participate in politics. Latter-day Saint scripture states, "We believe in being subject to kings, presidents,

rulers, and magistrates, in obeying, honoring, and sustaining the law" (A of F 12). Being an honorable, law-abiding citizen of whatever country in which they live is more than a civic duty. To Latter-day Saints, it is a religious obligation—a matter of spiritual commitment. This results in encouragement for involvement at all levels of government service as well as serving in the military. The Church remains politically neutral on all but a few political issues deemed moral in nature. Many conservative Church members are affiliated with the Republican Party in the United States, and numerous who care deeply about social justice issues are Democrats. Mormons believe that "he that keepeth the laws of God hath no need to break the laws of the land" (D&C 58:21).

## Watch Care

A uniquely Mormon service program is called Home Teaching. Every family is assigned two home teachers, usually an older man and a youth between 12 and 18 years old, who have a few

◄ *The average educational level of Mormons is above national norms in the United States.*

▶ *Senior Mormon couples will often serve a six-month to two-year Church mission following retirement.*

▼ *Mormons are well known for helping with community needs wherever they live.*

## Polygamy Not Practiced by Mormons

A curiosity in Mormon history is polygamy, or plural marriage. It was only practiced for about 50 years, primarily in the mid-to-late 1800s. Polygamy, as practiced by Old Testament prophets, Abraham, Jacob, Moses and others, was restablished by Joseph Smith in 1842 as part of the restoration of "all things" in the "dispensation of the fulness of times" (see Eph. 1:10). Plural marriage was not viewed by Mormons as a promiscuous practice, but was an institution intended for the multiplication of offspring, and provided for the rapid growth of Church population during the pioneer period.

A tide of public intolerance led the national government to pass a series of measures, beginning in 1862, to halt the practice of polygamy. Faced with very stringent measures in the late 1880s, Wilford Woodruff, fourth President of the Church, ended polygamy in 1890 by stating in an inspired "Manifesto" that the practice was discontinued and that Mormons should follow the laws of the land. The abolition of the practice paved the way for Utah's entrance to the Union as a state in 1896.

Polygamy has not been practiced by Mormons for more than 120 years. Some splinter groups not associated with the Mormons still practice polygamy and are sometimes confused with the LDS Church. Mormons follow the teaching from the Book of Mormon that, unless God reveals otherwise, a man should have but "one wife; and concubines he shall have none" (Jacob 2:27, 30).

families to visit once a month, to whom they give a short lesson taken from the *Ensign,* which is the Church monthly magazine in English-speaking countries (called the *Liahona* elsewhere). The very first article in each issue of the magazine is a message from either the President of the Church or one of his two counselors in the First Presidency. Home teachers also check to see whether the family has any needs that they or other Church members can help resolve.

A parallel program, visiting teaching, is especially for women. Adult women in the Church are assigned two visiting teachers. They, too, visit once a month and give a short lesson, as well as asking about any needs the women may have. Home teachers and visiting teachers often become good friends with those they visit and offer considerable help with such things as installing a new roof or perhaps helping to resolve personal or family problems that may arise from time to time.

## Temple Attendance

By the end of 2012, there were 140 temples in operation around the world. About 30 more had been announced or

▲ *LDS women have visiting teachers who come once a month with a short lesson and offer any needed support.*

▶ *Home teachers visit once a month with a brief lesson, and try to help with individual or family needs.*

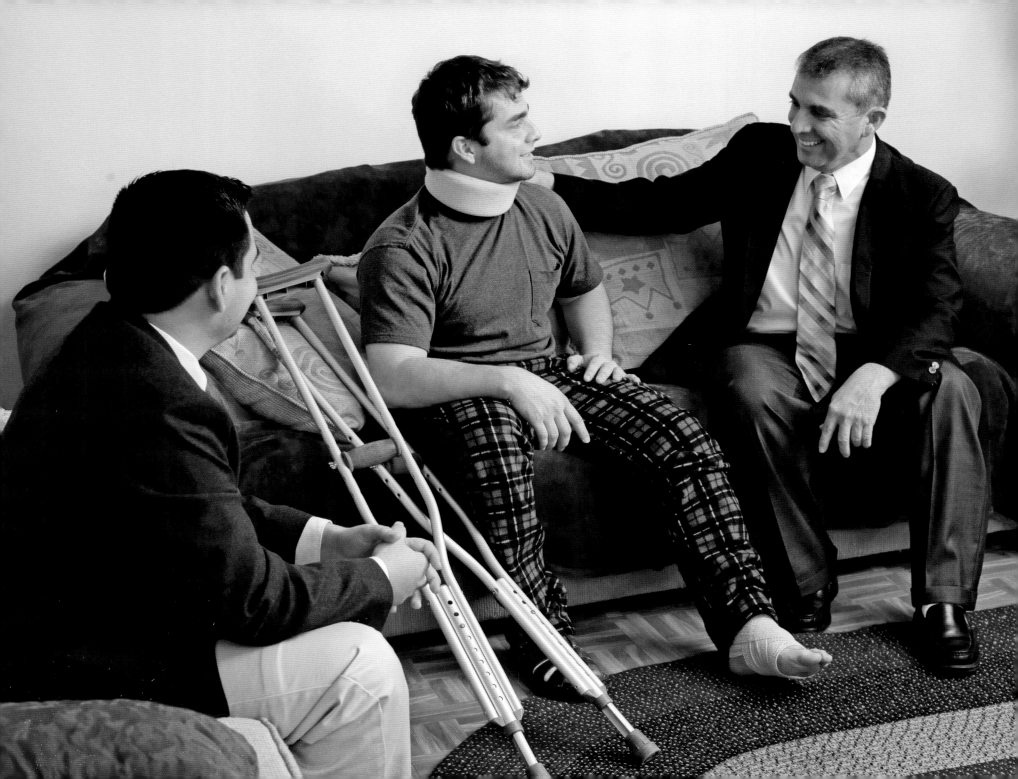

were in various stages of completion. Temples are important to Latter-day Saints for at least two reasons: There they may participate in worship services for their own benefit and spiritual strength; they may also receive rites and ordinances for family members and others who passed away without the benefit of baptism, confirmation, priesthood ordination (for males), the endowment rite (designed for increasing spiritual strength), and temple sealing uniting them as couples or as family units for all eternity. Non-members are invited to attend open houses in new temples, but once they are dedicated, temples are reserved for members in good standing. Temples are usually open to Latter-day Saints from Monday to Saturday. They are closed Sundays, when members attend regular worship services in Mormon chapels and other venues.

To be allowed to enter a temple, members must be interviewed by two local Church leaders every two years in order to qualify to hold a "temple recommend" (a scannable, paper document the size of a credit card). The interviews feature private, personal questions about one's faith and commitment to gospel principles and behavior. The possession and use of a temple recommend is seen as tangible evidence of fidelity to God and His plan of salvation for His children.

### Demographics

By 2012, there were more than 14,400,000 Mormons worldwide. About 43 percent of them live in the United States and Canada. Almost 2 percent of Americans (1 in 51) are Latter-day Saints—more than 6 million all told. There are large concentrations of Latter-day Saints in Mexico, Brazil, and other Latin American countries. Worldwide, there are 2,900 stakes, or ecclesiastical units similar to a diocese in many churches.[7] A stake usually has from 3,000 to 5,000 members.

*◄ The San Salvador El Salvador Temple. LDS Temples are designed to build spiritual strength through instruction and ordinances.*

*▼ Only worthy Church members are admitted to temples, which are deemed sacred places after dedication. After meeting for interviews with two Church leaders, members receive a temple recommend, which certifies that they are worthy to enter the temple.*

Within each stake are wards, or local congregations, usually having 200 to 500 people each.

There are about 19,000 Mormon meetinghouses around the world. Most serve more than one congregation, and Sunday meetings usually start at 9:00 a.m., 11:00 a.m., or 1:00 p.m. They are open to the public. Latter-days Saints tend to wear their "Sunday best," with most of the men in suits or sport coats, and the women in dresses. Families sit together in the worship service.

### Singles

Mormon singles, in spite of being unmarried, are usually very active in the Church. While some wards and stakes have been organized to meet the needs of those primarily in the 18-30 year old range (called young single adults in the Church), older singles generally attend regular wards where they participate fully and enjoy Church callings, teaching and leading in various auxiliaries and organizations.

Unmarried adults often organize Sunday evening meetings as well as other social gatherings where they enjoy each other's company. These gatherings may involve many singles from several stakes in a region and may feature speakers addressing interesting topics, scripture study, dances, barbeques, and other get-togethers that allow for social and spiritual interaction. Such activities often lead to marriage and sometimes the consequential blending of families where divorce has occurred.

All of the activities and programs of the Church are intended to produce Christ-centered lives, so that members and their children may enjoy the full blessings of the gospel, both in this life and in the world to come.

Those wishing to learn more about Mormons and their beliefs are welcome to attend a Sunday meeting or refer to a Church website such as http://mormon.org. Many resources for members can be found at http://lds.org.

**Notes**

1   "Mormons in America: Certain in Their Beliefs, Uncertain of Their Place in Society" POLL, January 12, 2012, http://www.pewforum.org/Christian/Mormon/mormons-in-america-executive-summary.aspx#family.
2   Ibid.
3   "The Family: A Proclamation to the World," *Ensign,* November 1995, 102.
4   Ibid.
5   Stan L. Albrecht, "The Consequential Dimension of Mormon Religiosity" in *Latter-Day Saint Social Life, Social Research on the LDS Church and its Members* (Provo, Utah: BYU Religious Studies Center, 1998), 286.
6   Ram Cnaan and others, "Called to Serve: The Prosocial Behavior of Active Latter-day Saints" (draft), 16; quoted by Dallin H. Oaks, "Sacrifice." http://www.lds.org/general-conference/2012/04/sacrifice?lang=eng.
7   2011 *Deseret News Church Almanac* (Salt Lake City: *Deseret News,* 2011), 308.

◄ *Sunday meetings are led by the bishop, a congregation member, called for a period of five-to-seven years. Bishops and other Church leaders serve without financial remuneration.*

# Education: A High Priority

Mary Jane Woodger

◄ *Students at The Church of Jesus Christ of Latter-day Saints' Brigham Young University in Provo, Utah, during a class break.*

▼ *The Church's Seminary program for high-school-age students provides weekday religious instruction for youth. Seminary curriculum focuses on the standard works of scripture used by the Church.*

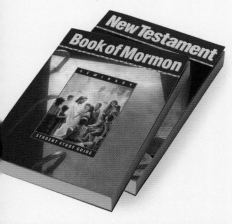

THE CHURCH OF JESUS CHRIST OF LATTER-DAY SAINTS has always made the education of its members a high priority and part of its mission. Many scriptural passages in its theology support this doctrine. Those that emphasize the importance of education include: "If a person gains more knowledge and intelligence in this life . . . he will have so much the advantage in the world to come" (D&C 130:19). "It is impossible for a man to be saved in ignorance" (D&C 131:6). "Study and learn, and become acquainted with all good books, and with languages, tongues, and people" (D&C 90:15). "I give unto you a commandment that you shall teach one another the doctrine of the kingdom" (D&C 88:77). And the ultimate LDS teaching that "the glory of God is intelligence, or, in other words, light and truth." (D&C 93:36)

## History

Early Church leaders did not differentiate between secular and religious education. Viewing education as part of the objective of The Church of Jesus Christ of Latter-day Saints, the first prophet, Joseph Smith, developed educational programs immediately after the Church was organized. In 1833, the School of the Prophets was established at the Church's headquarters in Kirtland, Ohio. It was one of the first schools ever designated for adults in the United States. The Church education classes for children and adults were continued when the Church moved as a body from Ohio to Missouri, then to Illinois, and finally to the Intermountain West.

As the Mormon pioneers entered the Salt Lake Valley, the Prophet Brigham Young quickly identified the education of children as a top priority. Although he said he never went to school until he got into Mormonism, his priorities for early pioneers were to first build a fort for protection from the Indians, second build a place for worship, and third build a school for the education of children.[1] As Latter-day Saints began to colonize western North America, they often set up community or ward schools. By the turn of the century, there were Church-run elementary schools in 375 settlements, stretching from Canada to Mexico.[2]

Beginning in 1875, a series of academies or schools for secondary students were established. To govern them, the General Church Board of Education was created in 1888 (later to become the Church Education System).[3] These academies taught both LDS theology and secular subjects. However, with the growth of tax-supported public high schools in the first two

▲ *High school students attend a released-time seminary class in a Church-owned building adjacent to their high school campus.*

decades of the 1900s, enrollment declined, and LDS academies were replaced by universities, seminaries, institutes, and continuing education programs.

For Latter-day Saints in Latin America and the Pacific, where public elementary and secondary schools were unavailable, the Church provided them during the twentieth century. As public education advanced in these regions, the Church-owned schools decreased. The Church still runs a few such schools: 16 in the Pacific and two in Mexico, with a student population of 9,255.[4]

Today the Church Educational System (CES) operates throughout the world through four main programs: religious education (seminaries and institutes of religion), higher education (universities and colleges), elementary and secondary schools, and continuing education.[5]

## Seminaries

During the twentieth century, with fewer Church-sponsored schools in existence, there was a concern that the Church's young people be taught the LDS gospel as part of their education. Accordingly, a new educational program was established, called Seminary. The first of these seminaries opened in 1912 with a few classes, 70 students, and one teacher in a small house adjacent to Granite High School in Salt Lake City. The program quickly expanded and became known as released-time seminary, with students attending gospel study classes during their secular school day. Today, released-time seminary is available in parts of Arizona, Colorado, Idaho, Nevada, New Mexico, Oregon, Utah, Washington, Wyoming, and Alberta, Canada.

In 1950, the first early-morning seminary was begun in California, with classes held in nearby Church meetinghouses before public school began. Twelve years later, this same program was expanded to Finland, Germany, Canada, Mexico, and the rest of the United States. Early-morning students now make up about 58 percent of all seminary enrollments.

In 1967, a seminary program was developed for LDS students living in rural areas, where released-time or early-morning seminary was unavailable. In such areas, students enrolled in a home-study program. By 1970, this program was available worldwide. Home-study students are assigned scripture study and other coursework in the curriculum and then meet with fellow students and a teacher once a week to discuss what they have learned. The purpose of each of these seminary programs is "to help the youth and young adults of the Church to understand and rely on the teachings and Atonement of Jesus Christ, to qualify for the blessings of the temple and to prepare themselves and their families and others for eternal life with their Father in Heaven."[6]

## The Honor Code

Students at Church-sponsored universities agree to live an honor code which includes the following:

- Be honest

- Live a chaste and virtuous life

- Obey the law and all campus policies

- Use clean language and respect others

- Abstain from alcoholic beverages, tobacco, tea, coffee and substance abuse

- Participate regularly in church services

- Observe the university dress and grooming standards.

▲▲ (Top) Brigham Young University-Idaho students participate in a forum assembly at the BYU-Idaho Center.

▲ Students at the Church College of Fiji in June 1980.

▶ The campus of Brigham Young University-Hawaii in Laie, Hawaii.

## Higher Education

The Church of Jesus Christ of Latter-day Saints owns and operates four institutions of higher learning. Together they have an enrollment of 45,000 students, with an additional 472,000 studying through continuing-education programs. These four institutions are LDS Business College in Salt Lake City, Utah; Brigham Young University (BYU) in Provo, Utah; BYU-Hawaii in Laie, Hawaii; and BYU-Idaho in Rexburg, Idaho.[7]

The primary purpose of the business college is to provide career-based education along with general-education degrees so that students can transfer to other colleges or universities. Brigham Young University is primarily an undergraduate teaching institution, although significant research is done by professors with undergraduate and graduate students. BYU-Hawaii offers undergraduate degrees and has the highest percentage of international students

enrolled of any university in the United States; one of its primary missions is to balance culture and diversity. BYU-Idaho, the most recent of the four, transitioned from being the two-year Ricks College to a full four-year baccalaureate degree-granting university. The primary role of BYU-Idaho is to teach, and its research focus is to improve teaching.[8]

Church resources allocated to higher education represent the largest single expenditure of The Church of Jesus Christ of Latter-day Saints, evidence of the Church's great dedication to education. These flagship Church universities represent a unique situation, combining "intensive religious scholarship" and "teaching of secular subjects in an atmosphere of faith."[9] "The educational chemistry on BYU's campus, therefore, involves a committed, competent faculty; a committed, competent staff; a committed, competent administration; a special student body; and, certainly, a special governing board. These groups are united on basic values and purposes—an academic adhesive that holds fast under pressure. The blend of these things permits BYU to do uncommon things that cannot be done as easily or as well elsewhere."[10]

◄ *The Carillon Bell Tower on the campus of Brigham Young University in Provo, Utah.*

▶ *The BYU cheerleading squad in Provo.*

▲ *Dusk on the BYU Provo campus.*

▶ *A performance of BYU's world-renowned International Folk Dance Ensemble.*

▶▶ *Classroom and graduation-day scenes at Brigham Young University.*

▲ *David O. McKay became the first President of The Church of Jesus Christ of Latter-day Saints to have completed a university education. Under his leadership from 1951 to 1970, Church education flourished.*

## David O. McKay

In 1919, David O. McKay, an educator and a member of the Quorum of the Twelve Apostles, became the Church Commissioner of Education. He later became the first President of the Church to have a university education. McKay taught that The Church of Jesus Christ of Latter-day Saints not only offered educational opportunities but embodied education itself.

It was under McKay's direction that a decision was made to either close or transfer most of the LDS schools to local governments when public education became more available. Some of the original academies still operating today include the University of Deseret (University of Utah) and Brigham Young College (Utah State University). The Church Education System continues to operate four of the original schools: Brigham Young Academy (now BYU), Bannock Stake Academy (now BYU-Idaho), Salt Lake Stake Academy (now LDS Business College), and the Juarez Academy in Mexico.

BYU alumni, who now exceed 400,000 individuals, apply the gospel principles they have learned to their professions and communities throughout the world. Every year more than 8,000 graduates make contributions to both the Church and the world. BYU faculty also have a worldwide influence through "publications, research, discoveries, inventions, and creations. They have leadership positions in professional organizations, and they collaborate with other scholars, participate in faculty exchanges, and host educational, political, and business leaders on campus. . . . BYU initiatives have often . . . open[ed] positive relations with other nations for both the Church and the United States."[11]

National acclaim has come to BYU as its 30,000 students espouse Church standards. For instance, *US News and World Report* ranked BYU the second most popular national university in the county.[12] The *Princeton Review* established BYU as its number one "Stone-cold Sober School," and BYU has also been declared the safest campus in America with more than 20,000 students.

▶ *During his senior year, BYU's Jimmer Fredette was the leading scorer in all of NCAA Division I basketball and earned every major National Player of the Year honor, including the Wooden Award, the Naismith Award, the Adolph Rupp Trophy, and the Oscar Robertson Trophy.*

▼ *BYU's popular Young Ambassadors performing group often tours the US and other parts of the world.*

The aim of BYU's athletic program is to "develop student-athletes of excellence in academics, athletics, faith, and character, and to contribute to the mission of the LDS Church through the visibility of our positive example and our accomplishments."[13] BYU's intercollegiate program of 10 men's teams and 11 women's teams has become one of the United States' top athletic programs, repeatedly receiving national rankings and recognition.

BYU male teams have claimed NCAA Championships in volleyball (1999, 2001, 2004), football (1984), golf (1981), and outdoor track (1970), as well as two NIT Championships in basketball (1951, 1966). BYU women's teams have won four NCAA titles in cross country (1997, 1999, 2001, 2002) and also have four runner-up finishes. In 2001, the women's basketball team advanced to the Sweet 16 at the NCAA Tournament, and in 2003 the women's soccer team made a run to the Elite Eight. Individual BYU athletes have also received national awards and recognition, including a Heisman Trophy, Doak Walker Award, two Outland Trophies, and two national basketball player-of-the-year awards. In addition, many BYU athletes have won national player-of-the-year or MVP honors.[14]

## Institutes of Religion

Because the Church universities cannot enroll all of the Church's young adults, the Church has also been involved in providing religious education to LDS students attending other institutions of higher education. In 1926, the Church began its first institute class near the campus of the University of Idaho in Moscow, Idaho. Since then, it has built similar institutes near other non-Church universities to offer classes to LDS students. The first international institutes were established in Australia and Great Britain in 1969. By 2012, institutes

were teaching more than 365,000 students at 2,214 institutes throughout the world.[15] There are very few places anywhere in the world where such classes are unavailable. Gordon B. Hinckley, former President of the Church, explained the purpose as follows, "In the institutes young college-aged students find happy association, they find learning, social experience, and even husbands and wives within the faith."[16]

## Continuing Education

The Church Education System also provides its members with a variety of continuing education programs, including Education Week, Especially for Youth (EFY), camps and workshops, and distance-learning courses which provide online or traditional correspondence courses for high school or college credit. In 2001, another continuing-education program, The Perpetual Education Fund, was established to support Church members internationally. It provides funds to Church members who have specific educational goals, with the aim of helping them break out of poverty through education and hard work.

## Making a Difference in the Lives of Millions

These four divisions of the Church Education System bless the lives of Church members not only by preparing students for professional careers, but also by helping them become better citizens, parents, and leaders.[17] Since its humble beginnings, the Church Education System's true accomplishments have not been "the size of the program or the numbers of buildings and teachers," but most important have been "the great things that have happened in the lives of millions of students over the years" because The Church of Jesus Christ of Latter-day Saints makes the education of its members a high priority.[18]

▲ *The education of its members has always been a priority for the Church.*

◄ *LDS Institute students take religion courses near their college campus.*

## Notes

1   Brigham Young, *Journal of Discourses*, 26 vols. (Liverpool: F. D. & S. W. Richards, Reprint 1967), 1:163-70.
2   The Church of Jesus Christ of Latter-day Saints, "Seminaries and Institutes of Religion Annual Report for 2011" (Salt Lake City: The Church of Jesus Christ of Latter-day Saints, 2011), 2.
3   Walter Cooley, "CES: Teaching Members Diligently," *Deseret News/Church News*, September 2005.
4   Ibid.
5   Ibid.
6   Marianne Holman, "100 Years of Seminary: Looking Back and Moving Forward," *Deseret News/Church News*, January 19, 2012, 13.
7   Cooley, "CES."
8   Ibid.
9   Merrill J. Bateman, "Conversation: The Role of Brigham Young University," *Ensign*, March 1999, 76.
10  Neal A. Maxwell, "Why a University in the Kingdom," *Ensign*, October 1975, 7.
11  Bateman, "Conversation."
12  Philip M. Volmar, "BYU Ranked No. 2 Most Popular School in America," *Deseret News/Church News*, January 30, 2012.
13  http://byucougars.com/athletics/mission-statement (viewed on May 4, 2012).
14  Ibid.
15  Cooley, "CES."
16  Gordon B. Hinckley, "This Great Millennial Year," *Ensign*, November 2000, 67.
17  "Education: A High Priority," http://www.lds.org.
18  Paul V. Johnson, Seminary Centennial Broadcast, January 22, 2012.

# Reaching Out to Those in Need

**Neil K. Newell**

10

◄ *On the first Sunday of each month members fast for two of their regular meals and give the value of what they would have eaten as a "fast offering" to help those in distress. Pictured here, two young men collect fast offerings.*

▼ *Church members are counseled to prepare for adversity by storing a three-month supply of food; saving money for emergencies; eating nutritious foods; growing a garden, where possible; and maintaining good health.*

IT WAS A ONCE-IN-A-CENTURY STORM THAT HIT Louisiana and Mississippi in late August of 2005. And when the winds, rains, and floods of Hurricane Katrina finally calmed, what remained was a scene of destruction and loss that could scarcely be imagined. The storm destroyed some 275,000 homes in Louisiana and Mississippi. It took the lives of more than 1,800 people and impacted more than 15 million others.

Immediately afterwards, people from all over the United States arrived and rolled up their sleeves. Among them were thousands of members of The Church of Jesus Christ of Latter-day Saints, who throughout the hurricane season of 2005 contributed some 336,000 hours of labor to anyone in need of a helping hand.[1] This army of Mormons descended upon the hardest hit areas—sometimes driving for more than six hours to get there. And armed with chain saws, shovels, and pruning shears, they worked 14-hour days, giving their help free of charge to any and all who needed it.

One woman, who had been desperately trying to organize a relief effort in her community center, watched as several vans drove up spilling out dozens of men and women dressed in their distinctive yellow shirts.

"Everybody! Everybody!" the woman exclaimed, her cheeks wet with tears, "The Mormons are here!"

## Succor the Weak

It is impossible to understand The Church of Jesus Christ of Latter-day Saints without understanding its commitment to reach out, lift, bless, and heal the lives of others.

In the first years after the Church was organized in 1830, new converts left their homes to be with the fledgling Church and be near Joseph Smith, the prophet of this new dispensation. Most arrived with little money and without a place to live. Joseph asked the Lord how the Church and its members could take care of so many hungry and homeless families. What proceeded was a series of remarkable communications that Latter-day Saints believe came from God. Members of the Church were commanded to reach out to those in distress: "Succor the weak, lift up the hands which hang down, and strengthen the feeble knees" (D&C 81:5).

From the earliest days of the Church, leaders and members have worked diligently to do as Joseph Smith taught: "To feed the hungry, to clothe the naked, to provide for the

widow, to dry up the tear of the orphan, to comfort the afflicted, whether in this church, or in any other, or in no church at
all wherever he finds them."[2]

The spirit of work, sacrifice, and sharing became an
identifying characteristic of members of The Church of Jesus
Christ of Latter-day Saints. During the 1930s, in the dark days
of the Great Depression, the people of Utah were hit particularly hard. With so many people out of work, Church members
and leaders pulled together to find land to till and orchards
to plant. Those who were employed worked alongside those
who did not have jobs—they all worked together for a common
cause. Soon, the food from these relief efforts began to fill the
cupboards and pantries of those who were hungry.

### The Modern-day Welfare Program

These early agricultural efforts were the beginning of the
Church's modern-day welfare program—a comprehensive

▲ *In 1936, the modern Church welfare program was created as a response
to the unemployment and distress created by the Great Depression. Pictured
here is the first cannery.*

▲ *Deseret Industries was established in 1938. Patterned after Goodwill Industries, Deseret Industries employs
some 6,000 people who have difficulty finding or keeping a job and works with them to reach their vocational
goals that lead to self-reliance. Seen above: one of 43 Deseret Industries stores located in seven western states.*

### The LDS Church Operates Many Facilities as Part of Its Welfare Program

The Church's welfare program was born
during the days of the Great Depression
and continues today as an efficient,
dynamic system that includes:

- 54 farms and orchards
- 143 storehouses
- 101 home storage centers
- 29 grain storage centers
- 327 employment service offices
- 43 Deseret Industries retail stores
  (second-hand store/donation center)
- 85 family service offices

In addition, the Church has built a range of
factories and other facilities to produce

food and household necessities for those in
need. These include:

- Soap plant
- Pasta processing facility
- Peanut butter cannery
- Bakery
- Flour mill
- Mattress factory
- Furniture factory
- Meat processing plants
- Milk and cheese processing plant

The goods produced in these plants are
available in the Church's many bishops'
storehouses (resource centers for the needy).

▲ Each year, the Deseret Bakery on Welfare Square in Salt Lake City distributes hundreds of thousands of loaves of bread to those in need.

▶ State-of-the-art, Church-owned canneries across the US preserve everything from peanut butter to peaches to salsa.

▶ ▶ Erected in 1940, massive grain silos at Welfare Square provide one of the Church's most enduring landmarks.

WELFARE SQUARE
THE CHURCH OF JESUS CHRIST OF LATTER-DAY SAINTS

system of caring for those in need. Canneries were established so that surplus produce could be preserved rather than going to waste, and so that food would be available during the cold winter months. Dairies and grain silos were built. Employment offices were set up to find jobs for the unemployed. Family Services offices were established to provide counseling and adoption services. By increasing the resources available over the years, the Church expanded the program enormously.

Most of the work performed in the welfare program is done by volunteers. Each year, some seven million hours are donated by Latter-day Saints who give up their evenings and Saturdays to work in one of the welfare facilities.

## Fast Offerings

One of the primary ways members of the Church help those who are in distress is through "fast offerings." Once a month, families go without eating two of their regular meals, and they give the value of those meals to the bishop (a lay leader over approximately 300–500 members). The money is set aside to be used exclusively to help those in need. There are no overhead costs associated with the fund, which means that 100 percent of the money given as a fast offering goes directly to those who most need assistance. Although some members of the Church give the bishop the exact value of the meals they did not eat, many give much more.

This fast offering has been a part of the Church from its earliest days when the Prophet Joseph Smith introduced it to help Church members who were not able to support themselves. The concept of the fast offering may go back even farther—perhaps even to Old Testament times (see Isa. 58:6–7).

A leader of the Church, former President Gordon B. Hinckley, said that if the principles of fast day and the fast

▲ *For more than 20 million people who can't walk, moving from place to place is only a dream. The Church of Jesus Christ of Latter-day Saints has provided wheelchairs or other walking devices to more than 400,000 people.*

◄ *The World Heath Organization estimates that 884 million people do not have access to clean water. The Church helps local communities to establish local water committees and provide hygiene training for families. More than 7.5 million people now have access to clean water as a result of these efforts in the past ten years.*

offering were observed throughout the world, "the hungry would be fed, the naked clothed, the homeless sheltered. Our burden of taxes would be lightened. The giver would not suffer but would be blessed by [this] small abstinence. A new measure of concern and unselfishness would grow in the hearts of people everywhere."[3]

## Self-reliance

Members of the Church believe that "when our wagon gets stuck in the mud, God is much more likely to assist the man who gets out to push than the man who merely raises his voice in prayer—no matter how eloquent the oration."[4] As a consequence, self-reliance has always been seen as a governing principle among the people.

Members who cannot make ends meet sit down with their bishop, who discusses their needs and resources and helps with their plans to become self-reliant. Each bishop knows the families and individuals and makes the judgment

about what kind of assistance is needed, whether it be food, furniture, counseling, job placement help, or housing. As part of this process, the bishop asks the various members of the family to do what they can to carry out their self-reliance plan. Sometimes, a family is able to do a great deal. Others may be capable of doing only a little. But how much or little does not matter. What matters is that they do what they can.

Because of this emphasis on getting people back on their feet, many members are able to become self-reliant quickly, and thus they can help others do the same.

All members are counseled to prepare for future adversity by storing a three-month supply of food—longer if possible—planting gardens, eating healthy foods, maintaining the best possible physical and mental health, and saving money for times of need. This emphasis on self-reliance and preparing for times of need have caused some to say that the "Mormons may be among the country's best prepared to weather the current economic hard times."[5]

▲ *Mormon missionaries and Japanese soldiers clean up a feed store that was damaged in the tsunami of March 2011. More than 22,000 Church-sponsored volunteers helped distribute 250 tons of supplies from the Church.*

▲ *Mormon missionaries and several hundred local members assisted in the clean-up after hurricane Sandy devastated parts of the eastern US seaboard in October 2012.*

## Humanitarian Work

The humanitarian work of The Church of Jesus Christ of Latter-day Saints reaches out to people throughout the world regardless of religion, race, sex, or political affiliation. Because of its ready store of food and needed emergency supplies, the Church is often among the first to respond in times of disaster. Along with their food, clothing, and medical and emergency materials, members of the Church are known for gathering by the thousands, eager to help those in distress in whatever way they can.

The Church has responded to hundreds of disasters—both natural and man-made. It has partnered with such respected charitable organizations as the International Red Cross and the World Health Organization, among many others, to bring help and hope to countless millions of people throughout the world.

Another of the distinguishing features of The Church of Jesus Christ of Latter-day Saints' humanitarian effort is that 100 percent of the money donated goes directly to help those in need. Overhead and administrative costs are supplied by a different fund.

The Church has identified specific areas of specialization when it comes to humanitarian relief :

- Providing safe, clean water
- Providing training in neo-natal resuscitation to doctors, nurses, and midwives
- Providing wheelchairs to those who have difficulty walking
- Providing food and agricultural training to the hungry
- Immunizing children against disease
- Performing eye surgery on those who have difficulty seeing and training other medical professionals to do the same
- Flying to the relief of the millions each year who are afflicted by disasters, both natural and man-made.

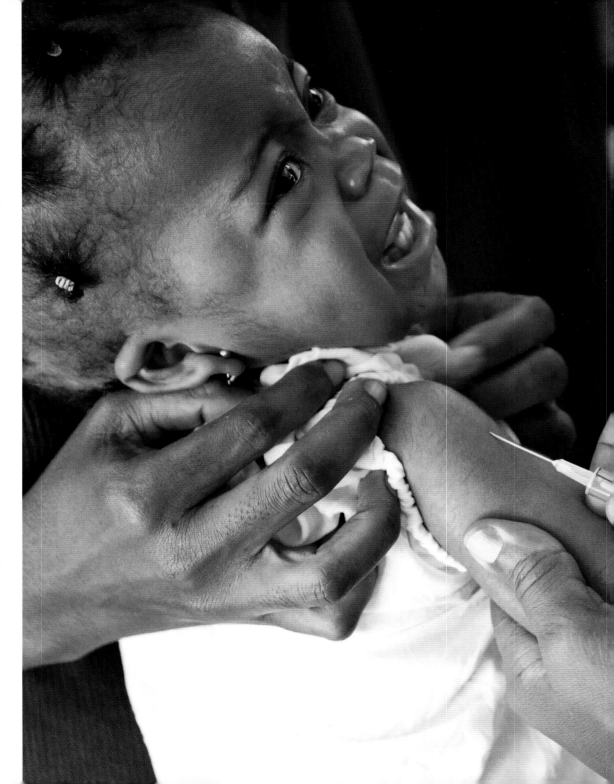

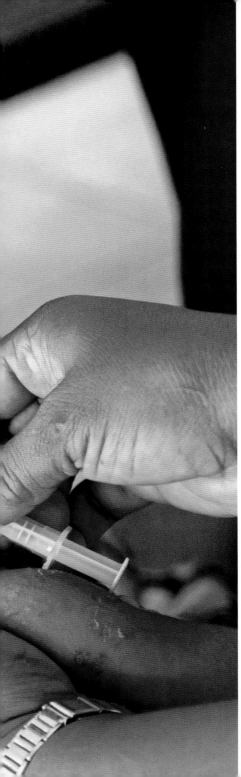

## The Great Commandment

For members of the Church of Jesus Christ of Latter-day Saints, caring for the poor is a covenant obligation and one the Savior listed as a "great" commandment (Matt. 22:39, 40). It is what the Savior did when He walked upon this earth. It is what He would have us do today.

The Prophet Joseph Smith told the fledgling Church in 1840, "A man filled with the love of God, is not content with blessing his family alone, but ranges through the whole world, anxious to bless the whole human race."[7]

From that day to this, members of the Church have given their time, resources, and material goods to reach out and lift up others in need. This act of charity is central to the disciple of Jesus Christ. It is the essence of the gospel.

It is one of the key things that must be known to truly understand The Church of Jesus Christ of Latter-day Saints and its members.

### Notes

1  See http://www.mormonnewsroom.org/article/mormons-work-with-communities-to-prepare-for-hurricanes
2  Joseph Smith, *Times and Seasons*, 15 March 1842.
3  *Ensign,* May 1991, 52–53.
4  Dieter F. Uchtdorf, "Two Principles for Any Economy," *Ensign,* November 2009, 56–57.
5  Associated Press, 2008, http://www.msnbc.msn.com/id/28392743/ns/us_news-faith/t/mormons-prepared-hard-times/#.T-t_A5Hud8E.
6  Marion G. Romney, *Conference Report,* October 1978, 131.
7  Smith, *History of the Church,* 4:2278. See also Spencer W. Kimball, *Conference Report,* October 1977, 123–24.

◄ *The Church provides funds for health education and immunizations. In the last decade, 60,000 Church volunteers have donated 766,000 hours to immunization campaigns in 25 countries reaching more than 100 million children on six continents.*

► *Members of the Church who are medical professionals (pediatricians, neonatologists, and nurses) go to areas of the world that have high infant-mortality rates and train doctors, nurses, and midwives to save the lives of newborn babies. In the last decade more than 190,000 medical professionals have been trained, who in turn are expected to train others.*

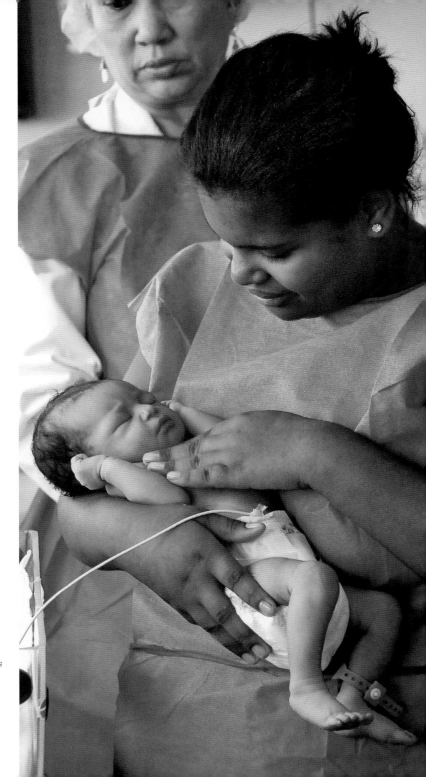

# 11

# *Mormon Temples Dot the Earth*

**Richard O. Cowan**

◄ *The Idaho Falls Idaho Temple, standing on the banks of the Snake River just above the falls, was dedicated in 1945. In temples such as this, brides and grooms make sacred marriage covenants, which they believe extend not only through this life, but into the world to come.*

▼ *One of the door knobs, created by pioneer artisans, on the east-facing facade of the Salt Lake Temple. The phrase "Holiness to the Lord" is inscribed on all Mormon Temples.*

FROM THE BEGINNING OF TIME, PEOPLE HAVE FELT the need to get away from the cares and materialism of the world and escape to places where they can ponder eternal truths and values. In many cultures, temples have been regarded as such places.

Beginning with the tabernacle of Moses, Old Testament sanctuaries had two major functions. First, like mountaintops, they were regarded as sacred places where the heavens and earth meet—places of revelation from God to man. Second, they were also where sacred rites or ceremonies were performed. Because they were regarded as sacred, admission to these precincts was limited. Mormons believe that both of these functions have been restored to the earth as part of the "dispensation of the fullness of times," as Mormons refer to the last days leading up to Christ's Second Coming.

The first Mormon temple was built at Kirtland, Ohio (near Cleveland), during the mid-1830s. The Latter-day Saints had overcome poverty and persecution to build the House of the Lord. As it neared completion, the Saints who met there enjoyed a rich outpouring of spiritual gifts, including prophecy, speaking in tongues, and visions of angels. Joseph Smith, the

founding Mormon prophet, declared this was a time of rejoicing, long to be remembered.

These events climaxed during the day-long dedication of the temple on Sunday, March 27, 1836. One week later, on April 3, Joseph Smith recorded that Jesus Christ appeared in glory to accept the temple, and that Elijah the prophet restored the sealing keys, which were "to turn the hearts of the fathers to the children, and the children to the fathers" (D&C 110). Thus, the Lord's house at Kirtland fulfilled the first of the ancient functions of temples—a place of revelation. Mormons see a connection between Elijah's "turning the hearts of the children to their fathers" and the organization, within a few years, of the first genealogical societies in both Europe and North America.

Sacred temple "ordinances" (ceremonies or rites) were unfolded while the second Mormon temple was being built at Nauvoo, Illinois. In 1840 Joseph Smith taught the Saints that they could be baptized on behalf of the dead, noting that the Apostle Paul had referred to this practice among early Christians (1 Cor. 15:29). The Saints eagerly waded into the Mississippi River to perform this ordinance, thereby making gospel blessings available to their loved ones who had died without this

◄ *Interior of the Kirtland Temple, showing multiple pulpits. Each level was for a different order of priesthood leaders. Latter-day Saints affirm that it was here that Jesus Christ appeared to accept the newly dedicated temple, and that the ancient prophets Moses, Elias, and Elijah, as resurrected beings, commissioned the Latter-day Saints to gather scattered Israel and turn the hearts of children to their fathers.*

◄ ◄ *(Far left) The risen Lord, appearing in the Kirtland Temple to Joseph Smith and Oliver Cowdery, declared, "Behold, I have accepted this house."*

◄ *The first Mormon temple, dedicated in 1836, is in Kirtland, an eastern suburb of Cleveland, Ohio. It was the scene of remarkable spiritual experiences at the time of its dedication.*

▶ *The Mormons' second temple was built at Nauvoo in western Illinois. Embodying some elements of classical architecture and surmounted by a 175-foot tower, it was a prominent landmark overlooking the Mississippi River. Before it was destroyed by the Mormons' enemies, baptisms for the dead and marriages for eternity were performed here. The rebuilt temple was dedicated in 2002.*

▲ *The Cardston Alberta Temple, dedicated in 1923, includes influences of Frank Lloyd Wright's architecture and has been recognized as a cultural landmark.*

## Why Do Latter-day Saints Do Vicarious Work for the Dead?

Latter-day Saints take literally the words of Christ when He said that the only way to enter into the kingdom of God is through baptism (John 3:5). But what about all those people who have lived and never had the opportunity to be baptized? Christ loves all people. Could He possibly leave them out?

When Christ atoned for our sins He set the example and laid a foundation for vicarious work—that is to say, work performed by one person in behalf of another. His atoning sacrifice was for all people who have ever lived. He literally suffered for our sins so that we would not have to pay the price.

Following this model, Latter-day Saints believe there is a way for all people to be baptized. Paul explained the concept in 1 Corinthians 15:29 when he spoke of baptism for the dead: *"Else what shall they do which are baptized for the dead, if the dead rise not at all? why are they then baptized for the dead?"*

Latter-day Saints perform baptisms by proxy for their dead ancestors. They find their names and when they lived; then they take or send these names to one of the temples. Church members actually go into a baptismal font and, as a proxy, are baptized for them.

But what if the deceased person wouldn't want to be baptized? One of the principles of heaven is choice. No one is forced to accept the baptism performed for them. They can accept or reject it.

That is why Mormons spend so much of their time doing family history research: they are offering their ancestors the opportunity to enter the kingdom of God, as if they had had the fullness of the gospel during their lifetime.

opportunity. In this way, God's plan for His children is truly just, because everyone has an equal chance to enjoy its benefits.

In 1842 the Prophet presented the endowment—a course of instructions teaching the path that leads back into the presence of God. Soon couples were being "sealed"— married with solemn covenants—"for time and for all eternity" (D&C 132:7–20). This represented a latter-day restoration of the second function of temples, a place for sacred priesthood ordinances.

Following the Mormons' famous trek across the plains to the Rocky Mountains, four more temples were built in Utah during the second half of the 19th century. The last of these was dedicated at Salt Lake City in 1893, having taken 40 years to

▲ *Surrounded by beautiful gardens, the Laie Hawaii Temple, dedicated in 1919, was the first Mormon temple outside of North America.*

◄ ◄ *The Manti Utah Temple, dedicated in 1888, is a landmark that can be seen from miles away. Each year an extensive pageant on the temple grounds, free to the public, portrays the story of the Book of Mormon and the beginnings of the Latter-day Church.*

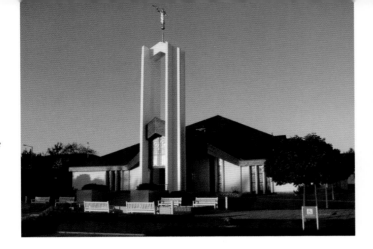

*◄ The London Temple, dedicated in 1958, lies in the countryside south of the city. Beautiful formal gardens were retained when the temple was built on the site of a centuries-old mansion. With the temples in Switzerland and New Zealand, this temple reflected the increasing international Mormon growth during the 1950s.*

*► (This page, left) The temple dedicated at Freiberg, Germany, in 1985 was actually behind the Iron Curtain. Communist government officials cooperated with the Church in building this temple, because they preferred that the Saints in East Germany receive their temple blessings there rather than traveling abroad.*

*►► (This page, right) The São Paulo Brazil Temple, dedicated in 1978, was the first Mormon temple in all of Latin America. When it was announced, Brazilian Saints rejoiced because they could afford to go to the temple for their sacred blessings. Formerly, they needed to travel to the United States.*

build. Atop the east-center tower is a statue of an angelic herald, Moroni, who in 1823 revealed the existence of the ancient record that became the Book of Mormon. Now a common feature of Mormon temples, these statues are seen as a reminder of the latter-day restoration of Christ's gospel and as a call to the faithful to prepare for the Second Coming.

During the first half of the twentieth century, temples were dedicated in Hawaii, Alberta (Canada), Arizona, and Idaho, reflecting the geographic expansion of the Saints. The Church's largest temple to that date was dedicated at Los Angeles, California, in 1956. During the 1950s, the first three "overseas" temples were erected, in Switzerland, New Zealand, and England. They were the first to use motion pictures in presenting the teachings of the endowment.

In 1968, Elder Thomas S. Monson, then a member of the Quorum of the Twelve Apostles, told a group of Saints during a visit to the German Democratic Republic: "If you will remain true and faithful to the commandments of God, every blessing any member of the Church enjoys in any other country will be yours."[1]

Seven years later, he offered a prayer of dedication on that land and its people, praying: "Let this be the beginning of a new day for the members of Thy church in this land," and he asked that their desire for temple blessings be fulfilled.[2] Dedi-

cated in 1985, the Freiberg Temple was the first and only temple constructed behind the Iron Curtain.

In 1975, plans were announced at a conference in Brazil for the first temple in Latin America. As a painting of the future house of the Lord was unveiled, a gasp could be heard throughout the huge arena. Tears filled the eyes of many as they wept for joy. This temple was dedicated at São Paulo in 1978. Two years later, the first temple in Asia was completed in Tokyo.

However, there were still many Latter-day Saints who lived thousands of miles from the nearest temple. Consequently, most could not take part in the solemn temple ordinances, such as sealing, to unite them as a family for all eternity. Some made substantial sacrifices to receive these blessings. For example, a Tongan family sold their livestock and went without new shoes and other necessities. For two years, all the children worked and saved, while the father rode a bicycle rather than driving a car, even long distances, so that they could go to the New Zealand Temple and be sealed.[3]

A man in Costa Rica who earned his living by selling food from a small roadside stand faced a difficult decision. He had only enough money to take three of his 11 children to the temple to be sealed, and did not know when he would be able to get back to have the others sealed too.[4] An even more difficult challenge faced the Saints in Korea, where the law made it

◀ *A radiant bride and a handsome groom before the San Diego California Temple. Belief in the eternity of the marriage relationship provides a sound foundation for young Mormon couples as they begin life together.*

▶ *The Washington DC Temple, dedicated in 1974, is one of the three largest Mormon temples and is a prominent landmark along the city's Beltway. Located adjacent to one of the world's major capital cities, it is a modern architectural reflection of the well-known Salt Lake Temple, with its two sets of three towers, surmounted by a statue of a herald angel.*

▲ *Mexico City has the largest Mormon temple outside of the United States, the fifth largest in the entire world. Dedicated in 1983, it has received awards locally because its architecture incorporates indigenous design elements.*

▲ *The Palmyra New York Temple, dedicated in 2000, is one of three Mormon temples built at Mormon historic sites. It overlooks the "Sacred Grove," where the founding Mormon prophet, Joseph Smith, had his vision of God the Father and Jesus Christ in 1820.*

▲ *The Accra Ghana Temple, dedicated in 2004, was one of two Mormon temples built at that time in West Africa. Because many Latter-day Saints in this area are very poor, traveling to the temple is still a significant sacrifice.*

extremely hard for a husband and wife to leave the country at the same time, making it nearly impossible for them to be sealed together as a couple in a temple.

## Taking Temples to the People

Clearly, having temples nearer to all these Saints would be a major blessing. During the 1980s, temples were built in such places as Tonga, Tahiti, Korea, Mexico, Guatemala, South Africa, and Sweden.

In June 1997, when Church President Gordon B. Hinckley visited the Mormon Colonies in northern Mexico, the concept of small temples came into his mind; they could be built more quickly and inexpensively yet could include all the essential facilities needed for temple ordinances. At a Church-wide conference later that year, he announced: "We are determined, brethren, to take the temple to the people and afford them every opportunity for the very precious blessings that come of temple worship."[5] During the next few years, these smaller temples, of

▶ *The Kyiv Ukraine Temple is the only Latter-day Saint temple to date, which was built within the former Soviet Union. Before its dedication in 2010, faithful Saints in the area needed to travel hundreds of miles to Germany to receive their temple blessings.*

▶ *The Kansas City Missouri Temple is one of the newest Latter-day Saint temples, dedicated in 2012. Situated only a few miles from Jackson County, from which the Saints were driven in 1833, it represents a new era of understanding and cooperation between the Mormons and their Missouri neighbors.*

▼ *Dedicated in 1996, the Hong Kong China Temple is unique among the world's Mormon temples. This single building includes a public chapel for meetings of the local congregation, administrative offices, apartments for the temple and mission presidents, as well as specific facilities for sacred temple services.*

which the Palmyra New York Temple is an example, were built on every continent. More than 60 dotted the earth. Nearly half of all Mormon temples are outside the United States.

Newly completed temples welcome visitors. In some cases, the response to this invitation has been so great that carpets had to be replaced before the temple was placed in service. After dedication, however, unlike Mormon meetinghouses where visitors are continually welcomed, temples are regarded as sacred places where only Latter-day Saints recommended as worthy by their local ecclesiastical leaders are admitted.

The 140th operating temple was dedicated in Calgary, Alberta, Canada, in October 2012. At that time, there were 28 others that were being planned or under construction.

Thomas S. Monson, who became President of the Church in 2008, said, "There are never too many miles to travel, too many obstacles to overcome or too much discomfort to endure. [The Saints] understand that the saving ordinances received in the temple that permit us to someday return to our Heavenly Father in an eternal family relationship and to be endowed with blessings and power from on high are worth every sacrifice and every effort."[6]

## Notes

1   Thomas S. Monson, *Conference Report,* April 1989, 66–67.
2   *Conference Report,* October 1985, 44.
3   Spencer J. Palmer, *The Expanding Church* (Salt Lake City: Deseret Book, 1978), 225–26.
4   LaRene Porter Gaunt, "Costa Rica, Rising in Majesty and Strength," *Ensign,* December 1996, 24–25.
5   *Conference Report,* October 1997, 68–69; see also *Ensign,* November 1997, 49–50.
6   *Deseret News/Church News,* April 9, 2011, 15.

▶ *Latter-day Saint temples may be found on every continent. They may be large or small, but are always of high quality. Mormon temples are sacred places where solemn ceremonies called ordinances are performed.*

BUENOS AIRES ARGENTINA

VANCOUVER BRITISH COLUMBIA

PAPEETE TAHITI

QUETZALTENANGO GUATEMALA

MADRID SPAIN

COPENHAGEN DENMARK

SEOUL SOUTH KOREA

PRESTON ENGLAND

APIA SAMOA

ASUNCIÓN PARAGUAY

MOUNT TIMPANOGOS UTAH

ADELAIDE AUSTRALIA

COCHABAMBA BOLIVIA

BERN SWITZERLAND

MANHATTAN NEW YORK

# 12

# *Family History and Genealogy*

**Kip Sperry**

◄ *The Church's Family History Library, adjacent to Temple Square in Salt Lake City, houses one of the most comprehensive collections of genealogical information in the world, with records on more than three billion deceased people. The library's resources are free and open to the public.*

▼ *People everywhere have a natural desire to know more about their family origins. Latter-day Saints also use family history research to find ancestors so that temple ordinances can be performed for them by proxy.*

GENEALOGY AND FAMILY HISTORY, THE SEARCH FOR one's ancestors and their lineages, has universal appeal throughout the world. It is estimated that nearly 20 million people in the United States alone are actively searching for their ancestors, and the number is growing.

What inspires such interest, even passion, in finding out about our ancestors? Alex Haley, the author of *Roots*, explained it this way: "In all of us there is a hunger, marrow deep, to know our heritage—to know who we are and where we came from. Without this enriching knowledge, there is a hollow yearning. No matter what our attainments in life, there is still a vacuum, an emptiness, and the most disquieting loneliness."[1]

In the quest to discover their roots, family history researchers examine family Bibles and read old journals, letters, and diaries. They visit archives, libraries, historical societies, cemeteries, churches, courthouses, and other repositories. They search census, church, and vital records, as well as court, military, probate, and many other kinds of records, in search of family history information. Happily, more and more genealogical resources, indexes, and services are becoming available online.

To assist researchers in their family history study, The Church of Jesus Christ of Latter-day Saints maintains the most extensive collection of genealogical records in the world. Comprising books, maps, microfilm, microfiche, numerous electronic databases, and other material from over 110 countries, these valuable resources are available not only to Mormons but to the general public as well. Millions of researchers utilize these free resources for their personal family history work.

## A Record-keeping People

Why does the Church make such an effort? Record-keeping has always been important to Mormons. On April 6, 1830, the day the Church was organized, Joseph Smith announced, "Behold, there shall be a record kept among you" (D&C 21:1). Since then, records have been kept of Church membership and history. Individual Mormons have also kept diaries, journals, and family records. Today, the Church's resources include biographies, membership records, census records for various years, computer databases and websites, indexes, vital records, and more—resources that are used by family historians everywhere.[2]

▲ *The Church has established more than 4,500 branch family history facilities in over 80 countries, with resources and volunteer staff to help members of the public document their ancestry.*

For Latter-day Saints, record-keeping is a sacred responsibility. They gather information about their ancestors so they can perform proxy (vicarious) temple ordinances for those who have died, thereby offering them the full blessings of the gospel. These ordinances are performed in temples. The first Latter-day Saint temple for ordinances was built in Nauvoo, Illinois. After the Mormon migration westward, the first temple to be completed was in St. George, Utah, in 1877.[3] As of October 2012, 140 operating temples throughout the world were being used by faithful Latter-day Saints to perform proxy temple ordinances for their deceased ancestors, with 28 more temples either announced or in various stages of construction.

### Record Gathering

In 1894, LDS Church President Wilford Woodruff emphasized the need for members of the Church to research their natural family lines. As a result, the Genealogical Society of Utah was organized in November of that year, and a library of printed genealogical materials was soon established.[4] This facility later became known as the Family History Library.

The Genealogical Society of Utah began microfilming genealogical and historical records in 1938,[5] and this records-gathering program continues today. The Genealogical Society of Utah now conducts operations as FamilySearch International, and its Family History Library collection includes over 2.4 million rolls of microfilmed records and more than 727,000 microfiche, containing the names of more than 3 billion deceased people. It houses over 356,000 genealogical and local history books, over 4,500 periodicals, maps, and atlases, and more than 3,725 electronic databases and resources. Records at the Family History Library include births, marriages, deaths, census population schedules, cemetery records, church records, compiled genealogies, immigration records, land records, local histories, military records, probate records, and many other genealogical resources.

### Easy Access

The Family History Library, located west of Temple Square in Salt Lake City, is open to the public free of charge. An estimated 1,500 people visit the library every day, some coming a great distance to utilize this extensive collection of genealogical and historical records.

There is another FamilySearch Center near the library in the Joseph Smith Memorial Building across from Temple Square. With computers, workstations, and a staff to help people search their family trees, this user-friendly resource also offers free family history services to the public.

Not everyone, however, can travel to Salt Lake City to research their family history at the Family History Library. As a result, the Church has established a vast network of over 4,500 branch family history facilities in over 80 countries around the world. Known as FamilySearch Centers, these

▲▲ *The Family History Library in Salt Lake City has an extensive collection of microfilm, books, maps, periodicals, atlases, and computer databases.*

▲ *The Church began photographing records in 1938, and continues today.*

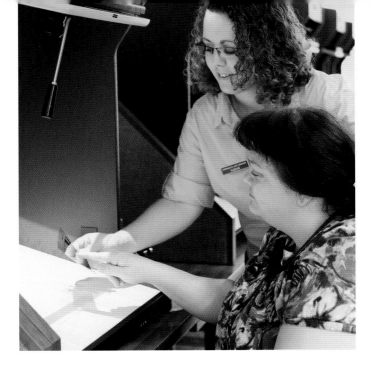

▶ *Volunteer staff at the Family History Library in Salt Lake City and at the 4,500 branch family history facilities across the world help individuals perform individualized research.*

▼ *The extensive microfilm collection of FamilySearch International is cataloged online. For a small fee, researchers can request that microfilmed records from the collection be sent to a local FamilySearch center for access on microfilm readers.*

facilities, often located in Latter-day Saint meetinghouses, offer many free services, including classroom training. Using the online FamilySearch Catalog, people can identify records from FamilySearch's collections they wish to study and can have these microfilmed records sent to their local FamilySearch Center for a nominal fee. When the films arrive, the researcher can use the center's microfilm and microfiche readers to review the records and gather information.

Those seeking their ancestors will also find a wealth of computer resources available at FamilySearch Centers, including an intranet web portal with free access to several useful genealogical databases, including Ancestry.com, the world's largest commercial database, and several other major genealogical websites.

## FamilySearch Website and Related Services

In May 1999, www.familysearch.org was introduced by the Church as a free family history Internet site. Several of its databases and research aids are available in multiple languages. FamilySearch is today the largest genealogical research organization and repository in the world.[6]

FamilySearch.org has several useful tools to help family historians with research. The FamilySearch Research Wiki contains a collection of family history articles arranged by localities and topics (such as US Census, and many others) and provides free family history research advice for the community, from the community. FamilySearch Wiki has become a growing resource monitored by many volunteer genealogical researchers throughout the world, and is available in several languages.

FamilySearch Forums are online discussion groups arranged by geographical localities and topics to provide free research and record assistance. At this forum, anyone—from

▲ *"Indexing" involves extracting data from images of historical documents.*

beginners to experienced researchers—can ask questions about FamilySearch product features, research techniques, or about specific families in specific localities. The forum is available in several foreign languages. Online volunteers answer patrons' questions, usually within 48 hours.

FamilySearch.org offers assistance, hundreds of free online research classes, a FamilySearch Blog, and Family Tree with lineage-linked genealogies for specific time periods and geographical localities around the world. The goal of all these services is to connect families across distance and time. The FamilySearch website also contains digitized genealogical records (such as census records, military records, probate records, vital records, and others), user-contributed family trees with lineage-linked compiled genealogies and pedigrees, personal name indexes, digitized family and local history books from several major libraries, and other online resources.

A related website sponsored by FamilySearch is FamilySearch Labs (https://labs.familysearch.org) where some of the most recent files and databases are displayed and tested, such as United States Research Assistance and Community

Trees. FamilySearch also has a presence on Facebook where useful videos and training aids are available.

## Granite Mountain Records Vault

To house and safeguard the vast genealogical records of the Family History Library, a storage vault was needed. The Granite Mountain Records Vault was built during the early 1960s for long-term storage of the original microfilms of the Family History Department.[7] The vault is located in a restricted area in Little Cottonwood Canyon southeast of Salt Lake City. It now houses approximately 2.4 billion images on 16mm and 35mm microfilm, maintained at carefully controlled temperature and humidity. This massive repository of international records from over 110 countries is the largest collection of microfilmed genealogical records in the world, with approximately 12 billion individual names. Most of the records date from the seventeenth century to the middle twentieth century.

## Digitization and Volunteer Indexing

To make these records more readily available, many of the microfilm images are currently being digitized and provided online at FamilySearch.org. FamilySearch continues to digitize original records throughout the world at the rate of approximately 75 million new images each year. In the FamilySearch indexing program, a growing army of online volunteers is undertaking the enormous task of indexing these newly digitized images. Indexing is done by individuals working at home on their own computers. Anyone with an Internet connection—Church membership is not required—can sign up and join the network of indexers. Over 400 million names per year are currently being indexed in this way. These personal names become part of online searchable databases, making more and more records available to researchers using FamilySearch.org.

Mormon young people, in growing numbers, are becoming involved in family history and indexing records. Because of their computer skills and their familiarity with other electronic devices and social networks, they fit easily into the modern arena of online research and are able to help those members of the older generation whose Internet skills are lacking.

## A Bright Future

The future of genealogy and family history research is bright. Currently, thousands of indexes and hundreds of millions of digitized records are available for anyone searching online at FamilySearch.org and at other websites. FamilySearch.org is growing rapidly. More and more records are becoming available, and increasing numbers of them will be digitally photographed, indexed, and accessible to researchers on their home computers, in many libraries, and in a global network of research centers. The Church of Jesus Christ of Latter-day Saints stands at the forefront of this explosion of genealogical resources.

## Notes

1 Alex Haley, 30th anniversary edition of *Roots* (Cambridge, Mass.: Vanguard Press, 2007), back cover. Haley also said, "In every conceivable manner, family is the link to our past, a bridge to our future."
2 Kip Sperry, *A Guide to Mormon Family History Sources* (Provo, Utah: Ancestry Publishing, 2007).
3 The first Latter-day Saint temple was built in Kirtland, Ohio, and is now owned by The Community of Christ. However, temple ordinances as later revealed were not performed there.
4 James B. Allen, Jessie L. Embry, and Kahlile B. Mehr, *Hearts Turned to the Fathers: A History of the Genealogical Society of Utah, 1894–1994* (Provo, Utah: BYU Studies, Brigham Young University, 1995), 42–47. See also *Deseret News 2012 Church Almanac* (Salt Lake City: The Church of Jesus Christ of Latter-day Saints, 2012), 302–03.
5 Allen, Embry, and Mehr, *Hearts Turned to the Fathers,* 216–21. See also *Deseret News 2012 Church Almanac,* 307.
6 Kip Sperry, "Salt Lake City: An International Center for Family History," in *Salt Lake City: The Place Which God Prepared,* ed. Scott C. Esplin and Kenneth L. Alford (Provo, Utah: Religious Studies Center, Brigham Young University; Salt Lake City: Deseret Book, 2011), 326–30.
7 Ibid., 330–32.

◄ *The Church's Granite Mountain Records Vault near Salt Lake City is an earthquake-proof repository of ancestral records from over 110 nations.*

# 13

# "Unto Every Nation"

**Richard O. Cowan**

◄ *After His Resurrection, the risen Lord charged his Apostles, "Go ye into all the world, and preach the gospel to every creature." This they did, "and preached every where, the Lord working with them" (Mark 16:15, 20).*

▼ *Samuel Smith, the first Mormon missionary, carried copies of the Book of Mormon similar to this 1830 first edition.*

FROM THEIR BEGINNING, LATTER-DAY SAINTS HAVE been a missionary-minded people. Their belief that The Church of Jesus Christ of Latter-day Saints represented a modern-day restoration of the New Testament Church of Jesus Christ and His gospel, in its ancient purity, has compelled them to share their faith with others.

Joseph Smith's younger brother Samuel became the first Mormon missionary. During the summer of 1830, he took copies of the Book of Mormon to distribute in nearby villages of western New York. From this humble beginning, the faith has spread throughout the world.

## Mission to England

By 1837, there were a few hundred Latter-day Saints, most of them living in the northeastern United States, in adjoining areas of Canada, and in western Missouri. In that year, the first overseas mission was opened in England—a group of seven missionaries led by Apostle Heber C. Kimball. On July 30, the first baptisms were performed in the River Ribble at Preston, Lancashire. By winning a foot race, George D. Watt gained the privilege of being the first of the multitudes who would join the new faith in Britain.

Along with their success, the missionaries had many moving experiences. When young children from the village of Chatburn came out singing hymns to greet Elder Kimball, he removed his hat out of respect and washed the tears from his eyes in a nearby stream. By the 1850s, there were more Latter-day Saints in Great Britain than in North America, and Mormon missionaries were carrying their message to Scandinavia and other parts of the Continent. Most of the early European converts emigrated to Utah and neighboring areas, providing a much-needed infusion of craftsmen for these frontier settlements.

## Expansion in the 1850s

In 1850, Mormon missionaries carried the restored gospel to Hawaii. They soon realized that they needed to know the Hawaiian language in order to share their message. On the island of Maui, the Hawaiian convert Jonatana Napela conducted a two-month language school for the American missionaries, providing room and board in his own home. For several hours each day, Napela had the missionaries read aloud from the Bible to become familiar with the sounds and meaning of the Hawaiian language. In the following decades, Latter-day Saint missionaries began to preach in other island groups.

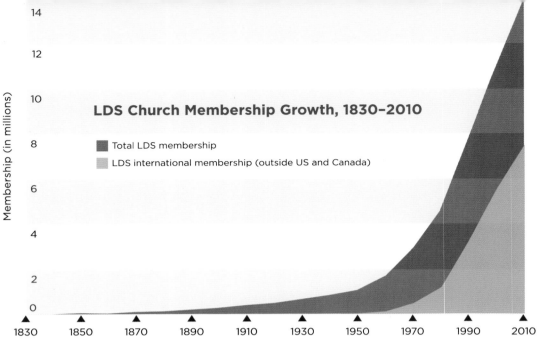

## LDS Church Membership Growth, 1830–2010

■ Total LDS membership
■ LDS international membership (outside US and Canada)

Membership (in millions): 0, 2, 4, 6, 8, 10, 12, 14

1830  1850  1870  1890  1910  1930  1950  1970  1990  2010

Missionary work flourished, and ultimately Polynesia gained the distinction of having some of the highest concentrations of Latter-day Saints anywhere in the world. For example, today nearly 50 percent of Tongans are members of the Church.

Meanwhile, Mormon leaders in Utah felt the need to share the gospel message with the whole world. At a special conference in 1852, they called for their members to go to such diverse places as British Guiana, the West Indies, Gibraltar, Hindostan, China, Siam, Australia, and the Cape of Good Hope. Even though most of the missions to these areas did not bear immediate fruit, they reflected the scope of the Saints' commitment to share their message with every nation.

### Mexico and Latin America

The first Latter-day Saint missionaries to Mexico arrived there in 1875. They attracted converts by distributing translations of selected passages from the Book of Mormon, which contained a history of the ancient inhabitants of America. But they had little success. A second endeavor in Latin America occurred fifty

▲ *The first Mormon missionaries to England enjoyed unusual success in small towns in the Lancashire countryside near Preston.*

◄ *Samuel Smith, the first Mormon missionary, was the younger brother of founding prophet Joseph Smith.*

▶ *Mormon elders serve in Polynesia.*

▲ *Following retirement, many senior missionary couples accept calls to serve around the world. The joy of sharing the gospel helps them sacrifice being with their grandchildren back home.*

◄ *Young women missionaries eagerly share their faith in many parts of the world.*

▼ *Mormon missionaries travel on their way to an appointment in Ghana.*

▲ ▶ *Missionaries serve in diverse places around the world, in rural as well as urban areas; in developed as well as developing nations.*

years later, when German immigrants carried their Mormon faith to Argentina in 1925. Church membership grew slowly at first but accelerated during the second half of the 20th century as Latter-day Saint missionaries proclaimed their message in an increasing number of countries throughout Latin America. Their efforts brought an abundant harvest of new converts. Significantly, the first two nations outside the United States to reach a Mormon membership of one million were Mexico in 2004 and Brazil in 2007.

## Asia and Africa

Ironically, wars were the means of introducing the restored gospel to Asia. Although Latter-day Saint missionaries first preached in Japan in 1901, the mission there was closed in 1924 when Church membership was only about one hundred. It was revived following World War II, when American Mormon soldiers shared their faith with the Japanese. For example, Airman Boyd K. Packer, a future Apostle, was instrumental in

teaching and baptizing the family of Tatsui Sato, who became a prominent leader. It was also military personnel who introduced the gospel just a few years later to Korea during the war there. The conflict in Vietnam then opened the way to establishing the Church in Southeast Asia.

Although Mormon missionaries preached in South Africa as early as the 1850s, the restored gospel was not introduced to most other parts of Africa until the last quarter of the 20th century. The introduction of the gospel into West Africa was unique in Latter-day Saint history. As early as the 1940s, individuals in this area wrote to Church headquarters asking for information. Then, during the decade following World War II, students from Ghana and Nigeria went to Great Britain, where they met Mormon missionaries. They returned home sharing their newfound faith with friends and neighbors. As a result, several groups in these countries—the largest containing more than 4,000 members—identified themselves as Latter-day Saints. These groups were bolstered by occasional visits to the area by Church members from America who came because of educational or business assignments.

For reasons that are not entirely clear—since Joseph Smith ordained some blacks to the priesthood—people of African descent were not admitted to the priesthood until President Spencer W. Kimball, after much fasting and prayer, and with the support of the Twelve Apostles, removed the restriction in 1978. This opened the door to missionary work in Africa. When official missionaries were sent to Africa in 1978, they found hundreds of people just waiting to be baptized. Africa has continued to have one of the highest Latter-day Saint growth rates anywhere in the world.

▲ *Mormons the world over, such as this group in Fiji, have faith that families can be together forever.*

◄ *At the Missionary Training Center in Provo, Utah, these missionaries are learning Spanish during a two-month intensive course.*

▼ *This map shows the presence of The Church of Jesus Christ of Latter-day Saints around the world.*

LDS presence

No formal
LDS presence

## Growth since 1945

Mormon expansion has not always followed the growth patterns of other groups. Typically, organizations grow the fastest when they are new and when enthusiasm is greatest. Latter-day Saint growth rates, on the other hand, have increased substantially over the years, particularly since the mid-20th century. As the 19th century tide of persecution receded, Utah entered the Union as a state in 1896, and by the first part of the 20th century, Mormon values such as honesty, hard work and clean living were widely appreciated. The strength of Mormon family life was frequently praised in the latter part of the 20th century, at a time when traditional family values and family structure had been eroded.

In the 1950s, Church President David O. McKay encouraged wider member participation in missionary work with the slogan, "Every member a missionary," and growth accelerated. The spread of religious freedom into more parts of the world after 1945 opened doors to missionary work in many more countries. In addition to growing more rapidly, the Mormon populations have become more geographically diverse. While less than 10 percent lived outside the United States in 1950, more than half of all Latter-day Saints resided internationally in the year 2000 (see graph on page 128).

Rodney Stark, a non-Mormon sociologist, anticipated this growth and asserted, "Mormonism may be the first important new religion to arise since Islam."[1] Sociologists of religion have made a distinction between sects and denominations. Sects typically are smaller, have higher standards of conduct than the general population, and grow primarily from conversions—a source of commitment and energy. Larger denominations, on the other hand, tend to blend in with the general population and grow mostly from natural increase (children being born to members). Even though the Latter-day Saints constitute one of the four largest faith groups in the United States, they have followed a different pattern.

Catholic sociologist Thomas F. Odea believes that the Mormons have avoided what he called "denomination stagnation" because of their higher standards and missionary emphasis.[2] Stark agreed: "Research has shown again and again that a defined moral beacon is part of what attracts many people to the church. . . . It's the strict churches that grow. . . . People tend to value religion for how much it costs. When it costs nothing they see through that. . . . If you ask something of people, you're apt to get it, and if you don't, that's what you get."[3] In recent years, convert baptisms have accounted for about two-thirds to three-quarters of Mormon growth.

## Missionaries Today

The army of Mormon missionaries, now more than sixty-five thousand worldwide, is the main engine driving Church growth. Most are young men, 18 to 21 years of age, who serve for two years, although young women and older couples also serve for shorter periods.

Local Church leaders interview prospective missionaries to determine their worthiness and ability to serve. The applications for missionary service are then sent to general Church officials, who review areas of the world where missionaries are needed and prayerfully consider how best to match available missionaries with a specific area.

The President of the Church then sends a letter to the future missionary, assigning him or her to a place and indicates the date of departure. Prospective missionaries eagerly watch the mail for this most significant letter and often open it with great celebration in the presence of family and friends. With

▲ *A native Bolivian missionary, who was himself a convert to the Church a few years earlier, baptizes a new convert in the waters of Lake Titicaca.*

▶ *Will Hopoate, an Australian rugby star, was willing to put his sports career on hold in order to serve a two-year Mormon mission.*

more and more areas of the world providing missionaries, it is not uncommon to have missionaries of diverse ethnic groups from far-flung continents serving in the United States—even in Utah, which is 68 percent Mormon!

Before beginning their service, missionaries report to one of the Church's dozen Missionary Training Centers for a three-week orientation in effective teaching methods and a review of key concepts to teach. Additional weeks may be spent learning a new language if necessary. Once in the field, missionaries spend most of their time teaching. A typical visit lasts about 45 minutes. The missionaries do not ask their contacts to buy anything or make a donation. They simply want to acquaint others with the Latter-day Saint faith. They may identify people to teach by means of door-to-door contacting, meeting people on the street, or through referrals from Church members. As well as teaching, Mormon missionaries regularly donate part of their time in community service or other humanitarian projects.

The goal is to share the restored gospel message in all parts of the world. Mormon missionaries are serving on all continents in more than one hundred countries. They do not proselytize in areas where laws prohibit the activity.

Missionaries pay their own expenses or receive help from family or friends at home. Usually this amounts to a few hundred dollars each month. They do not receive a salary or other financial compensation from the Church; they ask only for an opportunity to share what they regard as a precious and life-changing message.

## Notes

1  Rodney Stark, quoted in Richard N. Ostling and Joan K. Ostling, *Mormon America: The Power and the Promise* (San Francisco: HarperSanFrancisco, 1999), 262.
2  Thomas F. Odea, *The Mormons* (Chicago: University of Chicago Press), 1957.
3  Stark quoted in Carrie A. Moore, "Games, LDS Church Influenced Each Other," *Deseret News*, March 16, 2002, E4.

**Donny and Marie Osmond**

Donny and Marie Osmond (center) are members of a multi-talented musical family who have been on television since the late 1950s. The Osmond Brothers toured North America, the United Kingdom, and Japan, and Donny became a teenage heartthrob. Marie had a solo career, and during the 1970s was paired with Donny for *The Donny & Marie Show*. Donny and Marie have teamed up again in recent years in Las Vegas. The family has sold 102 million records and has started two charities: the Osmond Foundation and the Olive Osmond Hearing Fund. Marie Osmond co-founded the Children's Miracle Network which has raised 4.3 billion dollars since 1983.

The Osmonds—left to right:
Jay, Jimmy, Merrill, Marie, Donny, Wayne and Alan.

# 14

# *Mormons Who Have Made a Difference*

**Helen K. Warner, Michael H. Clifton, Carma T. Prete**

WHILE MORMONS MAKE UP ONLY TWO PERCENT OF THE POPULATION OF THE United States, a surprisingly large number have been highly successful. Noted author Stephen Mansfield suggests that their success is the fruit of their religion. Their belief in eternal life, he says, presents life as an obstacle course to be mastered. They have the advantage of strong family ties because of their doctrine that families can be eternal. The teaching that education and intelligence gained in this life continue into the next gives religious value to academic achievement.[1]

Members are taught from the cradle that "unto whom much is given much is required" (D&C 82:3). Talents are seen as gifts to be shared, so high achievers regularly lend their names to worthy causes.

# Arts and Entertainment ▶▶

Members of the Church are guided by Christ's teaching to "let your light so shine" and to offer their talents as an expression of their faith. Even small children are given opportunity to speak in meetings. Families perform together. Young people take part in choirs, dance festivals, and pageants. The Church programs offer a virtual stage for talents to be developed.

## Gladys Knight ▶

Called the "Empress of Soul," Gladys Knight is a legendary singer, songwriter, and actress. She has had numerous hits, the most famous being "Midnight Train to Georgia," and a long list of awards, including her induction into the Hit Parade Hall of Fame. In 1998, she joined the Church and has created the Saints Unified Voices, a choir of Latter-day Saints that won a Grammy Award for the CD *One Voice*.

### Stephenie Meyer ▶

Stephenie Meyer is a Latter-day Saint mother of three whose first novel, *Twilight,* spiraled to No. 5 on the *New York Times* bestseller list for Children's Chapter Books within a month of its release. Three novels followed, and the fourth, *Breaking Dawn,* sold over 1.3 million copies on its first day. Successful film adaptations have been made of the novels, which have been translated into 37 languages and have sold over 100 million copies.

### Don Bluth ▲

Don Bluth is an American animator who began his career with the Walt Disney Company and later teamed up with Steven Spielberg to make *An American Tale* and *The Land Before Time,* which are considered classics in animation. With Fox Animation Studios, he produced the highly acclaimed *Anastasia.* He is now passing on his skills with online tutorials in animation and drawing.

### ◀ David Archuleta

David Archuleta shot into fame in 2008 with his appearance on *American Idol* when he was 16. Each week he performed before millions on television and reached the final round of the competition as runner-up when the 97,000,000 votes were tallied. His first single on Jive Records sold nearly two million copies. He insists on singing material that agrees with his standards. He is currently serving a two-year mission for the Church.

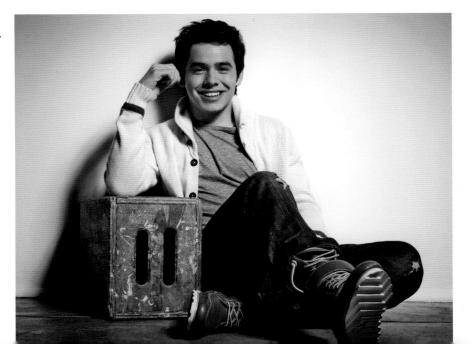

## Sports ▶▶

Mormon athletes have a definite advantage. They believe that their bodies are sacred and are taught to look after them. They follow a set of health rules that prohibit the use of drugs, alcohol, tobacco and even tea and coffee. Discipline, hard work, and clean living are enshrined. Theirs is a culture that encourages participation in sports from childhood. Most Church buildings offer sports facilities. Church schools have invested heavily in sports, and there is great recognition to those who excel.

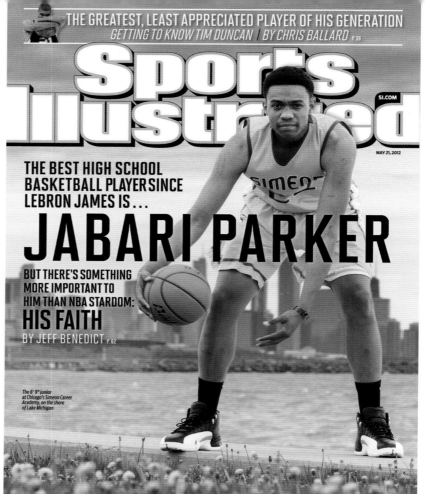

### ◄ Jabari Parker

Jabari Parker was named the USA Basketball male athlete of 2011 and 2012 Gatorade National Player of the Year. Still in high school, Parker led his team to a 33–1 record in the 2011–12 season. He honed his basketball skills playing most days on the court at the local LDS meetinghouse. He attends a religion class each morning at 5:30 a.m. and credits the influence of Christ in his life for his success.

### ◄ Peter Vidmar

Peter Vidmar is the highest-scoring American gymnast in Olympic history. As team captain, he led the 1984 USA Olympic gymnastics team to a gold medal in All-Around Competition; he then went on to win the silver medal in individual All-Around Competition, and another gold medal with a perfect score of 10 on the pommel horse. He has been inducted into the US Olympic Hall of Fame twice and has hosted the Peter Vidmar Men's Gymnastics Invitational for 21 years.

### Torah Bright ▲

Torah Bright is an Australian world champion snowboarder who has dominated the podium in women's superpipe and halfpipe events. She carried the Australian flag in the 2010 Olympic Opening Ceremonies and won the gold medal for Australia in the halfpipe. Bright has been widely quoted for sharing the fact that she is a Mormon. She does not drink, smoke, take drugs, or believe in pre-marital sex.

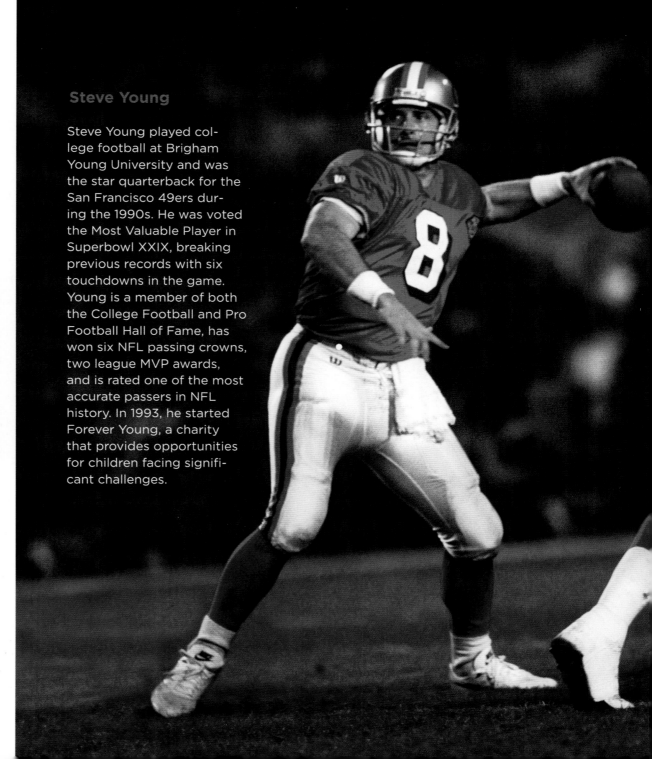

### Steve Young

Steve Young played college football at Brigham Young University and was the star quarterback for the San Francisco 49ers during the 1990s. He was voted the Most Valuable Player in Superbowl XXIX, breaking previous records with six touchdowns in the game. Young is a member of both the College Football and Pro Football Hall of Fame, has won six NFL passing crowns, two league MVP awards, and is rated one of the most accurate passers in NFL history. In 1993, he started Forever Young, a charity that provides opportunities for children facing significant challenges.

## Danny Ainge ▼

Danny Ainge has had an impressive sports career as a player, coach, and manager. An outstanding multi-sport high school athlete, Ainge became a top college basketball player. After playing major league baseball two years for the Toronto Blue Jays, he joined the Boston Celtics as a professional basketball player and was a star performer. Retiring as a player in 1995, he coached the Phoenix Suns for three years, after which he entered the Boston Celtics management team. He currently is President of Basketball Operations for the Celtics, and also serves as the lay leader of a local Church congregation.

## Dale Murphy ▲

During his 18-season major league career, Dale Murphy was National League MVP in 1982 and 1983, a five-time Gold Glove award winner and four-time Silver Slugger, and was selected for the NL All-Star Team seven times. He received the Roberto Clemente Award in 1988. Known for his good character and clean living, he continues to be an outspoken proponent of drug-free sports.

## Johnny Miller ▲

Johnny Miller is a professional golfer who was a 25-time winner on the PGA Tour, won two World Cups, both the US and British Open, and is a member of the World Golf Hall of Fame. After retiring, he became the lead golf analyst for NBC and has won eight Emmy nominations for Outstanding Sports Personality/Analyst. He started the Johnny Miller Junior Golf Association, a charity for young people.

# Business ►►

Commentators often attribute the success of LDS businesspeople to principles of hard work, discipline, honesty and thrift. However, observant Latter-day Saint businesspeople are most notable for personal sacrifices for their faith. They pay tithes and serve as lay leaders; they teach and assist individuals in need; some serve missions for the Church or support others who do so. Though they are not necessarily perfect saints, the gospel of Jesus Christ is central to their lives.

## ◄ Hyrum Smith

Former US Army field commander Hyrum W. Smith is not only named after the martyred brother of the LDS Church founder, but is also his great-great-grandson. Author of several books on life management skills and founder of Franklin Quest Co., Franklin Covey Co. (the result of a merger with Stephen Covey's Covey Leadership Institute) and the Galileo Initiative, Smith teaches that the key to satisfaction and success lies in conforming one's life to one's values.

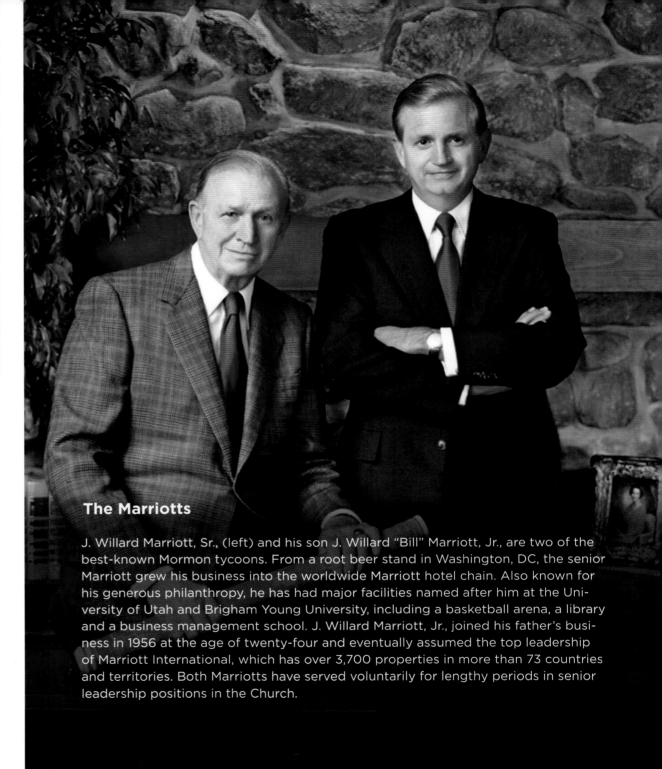

## The Marriotts

J. Willard Marriott, Sr., (left) and his son J. Willard "Bill" Marriott, Jr., are two of the best-known Mormon tycoons. From a root beer stand in Washington, DC, the senior Marriott grew his business into the worldwide Marriott hotel chain. Also known for his generous philanthropy, he has had major facilities named after him at the University of Utah and Brigham Young University, including a basketball arena, a library and a business management school. J. Willard Marriott, Jr., joined his father's business in 1956 at the age of twenty-four and eventually assumed the top leadership of Marriott International, which has over 3,700 properties in more than 73 countries and territories. Both Marriotts have served voluntarily for lengthy periods in senior leadership positions in the Church.

### ◀ David Neeleman

Brazilian-born American entrepreneur David Neeleman has been involved in the founding and/or leadership of numerous airlines, including Morris Air, Southwest Airlines, Jet Blue, and Brazil's domestic carrier, Azul. In a series of lectures for Stanford University, Neeleman explained his employee- and customer-focused approach to business leadership and his willingness to learn from others and from failure. A 2008 article on Forbes.com described him as "buoyantly optimistic."

### ◀ Gary Crittenden

Harvard Business School graduate Gary Crittenden is one of America's visionary business leaders, having held senior executive and director positions in several major corporations, including Sears Roebuck and Company, American Express, Citi Holdings, Inc., Citigroup Japan Holdings Corp., Staples, Inc., Ryerson, Inc., Reardon Commerce, Inc., The TJX Companies, Inc. and Utah Capital Investment Corp. Crittenden is CEO and managing partner of Huntsman Gay Global Capital.

### Stephen R. Covey ▼

In 1996, *Time* magazine named Stephen R. Covey (1932–2012) one of America's 25 most influential people. Through seminars and books such as the top-selling *The 7 Habits of Highly Effective People*—which has sold over 20 million copies—Covey has instructed a vast number of people about the keys to leadership in business, community, and personal life. Many of Covey's key concepts were derived from his religious beliefs.

### Jon Huntsman, Sr. ▶

Jon Huntsman, Sr., has lived a genuine "rags to riches" story. Born into a poor, Idaho family, he went on to become one of the world's 50 richest people, founding and leading Huntsman Chemical and H&G Capital Partners (now Huntsman Gay Global Capital). A noted philanthropist, Huntsman provides hundreds of millions of dollars to various causes, including the Huntsman Cancer Institute in Salt Lake City, Utah.

### Dave Checketts ▼

Once the youngest chief executive in the NBA as general manager of the Utah Jazz, Dave Checketts was later president and CEO of The Madison Square Garden Company, owner of numerous sports teams, networks, and facilities. He then started his own consulting and the investment firm, SCP Worldwide, which owns the St. Louis Blues, the Peoria Rivermen, Real Salt Lake, the Scottrade Center, and Kiel Opera House. Checketts also serves on the boards of several corporations.

### ◀ Alan and Karen Ashton

Not only a successful businessman, Alan Ashton is a computer software expert, merging both skills as the co-founder, president, and CEO of WordPerfect Corporation. He later formed the venture investment company ASH Capital. With his wife Karen, he founded Thanksgiving Point, a 52-acre Utah garden (including a museum, movie theatre, and golf course) where families can learn about farming, gardening, and cooking.

# Science ▶▶

Mormons believe that one of the purposes of life is to gain knowledge. They believe that God created and rules the universe using eternal laws, and in their quest to become like Him, they seek to discover and understand these laws. For Mormons, science and religion are not opposed—they are complementary—and the search for knowledge has led to remarkable scientific discoveries.

## Tracy Hall ▲

Tracy Hall (1919–2008), a physical chemist, was the first to produce synthetic diamonds using a verifiable and reproducible process and a press of his own design. He later invented improved diamond presses that produced industrial diamonds and drill bits. Dr. Hall was granted 19 patents for his work and received many prestigious honors.

## Philo T. Farnsworth

In 1927 Philo T. Farnsworth (1906–1971), inventor of television, transmitted the first television image using his all-electronic fully functional video camera tube. During his lifetime he was granted a total of 165 US patents and more than 100 foreign patents, mostly for inventions in radio and television. There is a statue of him in the US Capitol Building.

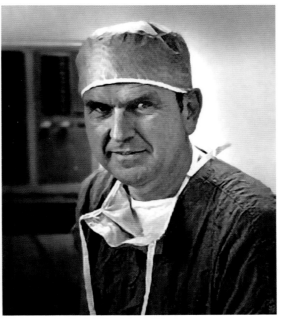

### Russell M. Nelson

Russell M. Nelson was part of a team that developed the first heart-lung machine ever used, and was the first surgeon to perform open-heart surgery successfully in Utah. He was a skillful and innovative surgeon who developed numerous improvements in cardiac surgery and received many professional honors. He served as a director of the American Board of Thoracic Surgery as well as receiving the Citation for International Service by the American Heart Association. He was later called to be an Apostle, one of the highest offices in The Church of Jesus Christ of Latter-day Saints.

### Henry Eyring ▲

Theoretical chemist Henry Eyring (1901–1981) developed one of the most important concepts in twentieth-century chemistry, the Transition State Theory of chemical reactions, or Absolute Rate Theory.  A prolific writer, Dr. Eyring authored more than 600 scientific papers and 10 books. He won the Wolf Prize in chemistry and the National Medal of Science.

### Harvey Fletcher ▶

Known as the "father of stereophonic sound," physicist Harvey Fletcher (1884–1981) is also known for his contributions to the theory of speech perception and hearing, and is credited with the invention of the hearing aid and the audiometer. During his long life, Dr. Fletcher was the recipient of numerous honors and awards, including the Louis E. Levy Medal for the physical measurement of audition.

# Government ▶▶

Mormons are taught to be law-abiding citizens wherever they live in the world and to be actively involved in their communities. Many hold prominent positions in government. The Church itself is politically neutral and does not endorse political parties or candidates, nor does it tell its members how to vote or act when they are in office. Mormons often have diverse political views. For example, 2012 Republican presidential nominee Mitt Romney and Democratic Senate Majority Leader Harry Reid are both active Mormons.

## Larry Echo Hawk ▼

Larry Echo Hawk resigned his post as head of the United States Bureau of Indian Affairs to serve as a Latter-day Saint General Authority in April 2012. A member of the Pawnee Nation of Oklahoma, Echo Hawk is an attorney, legal scholar, and politician who has championed Indian rights and causes throughout his career. A Democrat, he was the first American Indian in US history to serve as an Attorney General when he was elected in Idaho in 1990.

## ◄ Harry Reid

Harry Reid, Senate Majority Leader, is the senior United States senator from Nevada and has served since 1986. Representing the Democratic Party, he has had a distinguished career in both local and state government, was the twenty-fifth Lieutenant Governor of Nevada, and has served as Minority Leader and as both Minority and Majority Whip in the Senate. He authored and passed legislation to form Nevada's first national park and has a reputation for integrity and hard work. He once said "I am a Democrat because I am a Mormon, not in spite of it."

## Orrin Hatch ▶

Orrin Hatch is a six-term Republican senator from Utah. He is the ranking member of the Senate Finance Committee and serves on the Board of Directors for the United States Holocaust Memorial Museum in Washington, DC. One of his major contributions has been the passage of the Radiation Compensation Act of 1990, which provided compensation for Utah citizens injured by radioactive fallout from nuclear testing in Nevada.

## Jon Huntsman, Jr. ▼

Jon Huntsman, Jr., learned Mandarin when he served a mission for The Church of Jesus Christ of Latter-day Saints in Taiwan. His language skills were an advantage when he was called to serve as the US Ambassador to Singapore under the George H. W. Bush administration and as the US Ambassador to China under the Obama administration. He was the sixteenth Governor of Utah, and a candidate for the 2012 Republican presidential nomination.

### Notes

1   Stephen Mansfield, *The Mormonizing of America* (Brentwood, TN: Worthy Publishing, 2012), 30-38.

## Mitt Romney

Mitt Romney is the son of Michigan governor and American Motors president George Romney. After graduate degrees from Harvard, he co-founded the successful investment firm, Bain Capital. When the 2002 Salt Lake City Olympics became embroiled in scandal and financial woes, Romney was brought on as its chief organizer; and, working without salary or expense account, he turned it into a major success. He served one term as Governor of Massachusetts and lost the 2008 Republican presidential nomination to Senator John McCain. He was the 2012 Republican presidential nominee, running against President Barack Obama, but failed to win the presidency.

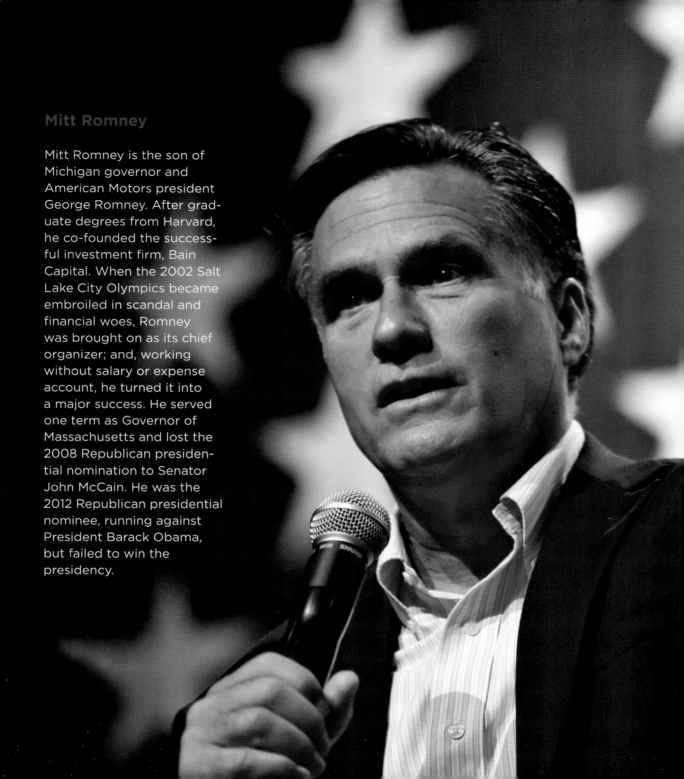

# Conclusions

MORMONISM CLAIMS TO BE THE RESTORED Church of Jesus Christ, an inspired update of traditional Christianity. Jesus said that "by their fruits ye shall know them" (Matt. 7:20). He also encouraged His disciples to be in the world but "not of the world" (John 17:15–16).

Mormons strive for holiness, to be apart from the world whose standards of ethical and moral conduct have often gone awry, yet to live in that world and participate fully. Their challenge is that of Confucius—how to be a good person in a bad world.

How do Mormons fit within the fabric of American religious culture and other cultures worldwide? Like other Christians, they believe in the Trinity, but not in a triune (or three-in-one) God; rather, in three distinct beings: God the Father, His son Jesus Christ, and the Holy Ghost. They teach that salvation is available to all through faith in Christ, by following His teachings and "by obedience to the laws and ordinances of the Gospel" (A of F 3).

Their affirmation of Christ is the core of their belief system. With all Christians, they believe that Jesus Christ was the son of God, and that through His infinite sacrifice, He ransomed mankind from their sins on condition of faith in Him and compliance with His commandments. They believe in the literal resurrection of all mankind. They baptize in water by immersion at the age of accountability and attempt to fulfill Christ's commandment to endure to the end by a life of devotion and service.

Some things set them apart. They entertain without alcohol and follow a health code that prohibits smoking, and even tea and coffee. They have more children than the population at large and have a family and church culture that is vital to their way of life. Their religion is so important to them that they routinely send their sons and many of their daughters into faraway lands to share their message, often with other Christians. Mormon missionaries are found everywhere in the world where there is religious freedom.

They believe that families can be together forever, and they have sacred temple rituals that join families together "for time and eternity." Through vicarious work for the dead, they perform ordinances such as baptism to extend salvation to previous generations who may have lived and died without knowledge of the gospel of Jesus Christ. They build temples all around the world for the performance of these sacred rites, but they also build churches which are open to everyone.

Mormons fit well into the general fabric of the many nations in which they live. They are patriotic, fight in wars as required, and serve with various political parties. They strive to be solid citizens in their communities, and they excel in many areas of endeavor.

They are part of the mainstream of Christian culture, but with some differences. While they have some distinctive beliefs and practices, their Christian discipleship is amply demonstrated by their faith in Jesus Christ and their commitment to following His teachings. Theirs is an integrated belief system and an integrated way of life that brings purpose, cohesion and deep meaning to many in a largely fragmented world.

▶ *As Christ ascended into heaven after His Resurrection, two angels appeared and said to the Apostles, "Ye men of Galilee, why stand ye gazing up into heaven? this same Jesus which is taken up from you into heaven shall so come in like manner" (Acts 1:10–11). Mormons, like other Christians, anticipate the Second Coming of Jesus Christ. Latter-day Saints view the restoration of the gospel as a preparation for the millennial reign, in which Christ will reign for 1000 years on the earth (D&C 65:2, 5–6).*

▶ *After His Resurrection, the Book of Mormon relates that Christ appeared to the inhabitants of the Americas. After teaching them His gospel, He blessed their children (see 3 Ne. 11–17).*

# For Further Reading

Alexander, Thomas G. *Mormonism in Transition: A History of the Latter-day Saints, 1890–1930.* Urbana: University of Illinois, 1996.

Allen, James B., and Glen M. Leonard. *The Story of the Latter-day Saints.* Salt Lake City: Deseret Book, 1976.

Arrington, Leonard J., and Davis Bitton. *The Mormon Experience: A History of the Latter-day Saints.* New York: Knopf, 1979.

Ballard, M. Russell. *Our Search for Happiness: An Invitation to Understand the Church of Jesus Christ of Latter-day Saints.* Salt Lake City: Deseret Book, 1993.

Black, Susan Easton, and Mary Jane Woodger. *Women of Character: Profiles of 100 Prominent LDS Women.* American Fork, Utah: Covenant Communications, Inc., 2011.

Bowman, Matthew. *The Mormon People: The Making of an American Faith.* New York: Random House, 2012.

Bushman, Claudia L. *Contemporary Mormonism: Latter-day Saints in Modern America.* Lanham: Rowman Littlefield, 2008.

Bushman, Richard L., and Jed Woodworth. *Joseph Smith: Rough Stone Rolling.* New York: Vintage Books, 2007.

Cowan, Richard O. *Temples to Dot the Earth.* Springville, Utah: Cedar Fort, Inc., 2011.

Cowan, Richard O. *The Latter-day Saint Century.* Salt Lake City: Bookcraft, 1999.

Ludlow, Daniel H., ed. *Encyclopedia of Mormonism.* New York: Macmillan, 1992.*

Ludlow, Victor L. *Principles and Practices of the Restored Gospel.* Salt Lake City: Deseret Book, 1992.

Plewe, Brandon S., ed., et al. *Mapping Mormonism: An Atlas of Latter-day Saint History.* Provo, Utah: Brigham Young University Press, 2012.

Prete, Roy A., ed., et al. *Window of Faith: Latter-day Saint Perspectives on World History.* Provo, Utah: Religious Studies Center, Brigham Young University, 2005.*

Richards, LeGrand. *A Marvelous Work and a Wonder.* Salt Lake City: Deseret Book, [C 1956] 1988.

* Books available online.

Robinson, Stephen Edward. *Believing Christ: The Parable of the Bicycle and Other Good News.* Salt Lake City: Deseret Book, 1992.

Shipps, Jan. *Mormonism: The Story of a New Religious Tradition.* Urbana: University of Illinois Press, 1985.

Sweat, Anthony. *Mormons: An Open Book.* Salt Lake City: Deseret Book, 2012.

▼ *During His appearance in the Americas, Jesus instructed the assembled multitude: "Pray in your families unto the Father, always in my name, that your wives and your children may be blessed (3Ne. 18:21)." In many Mormon homes, family prayer is a regular part of daily family life.*

# Contributors

**Susan Easton Black** is Professor of Church History and Doctrine at Brigham Young University. She has written, edited, and compiled over 90 books as well as many articles. In 2000 she was awarded the Karl G. Maeser Distinguished Faculty Award, the highest honor given to a professor at BYU.

**Michael H. Clifton** is a prominent lawyer, businessman, writer, and teacher. In addition to sitting on several boards, he is co-author of two books on Ontario condominium law and has published numerous articles on topics as varied as condominium development, Japanese history, art, religion, and politics.

**Richard O. Cowan** is Professor of Church History and Doctrine at Brigham Young University. Author of nine books and numerous articles, he has served as department chair and has taught at the BYU Jerusalem Center. He has received various honors, including BYU Professor of the Year and Phi Kappa Phi.

**John P. Livingstone** is Associate Professor of Church History and Doctrine at Brigham Young University, as well as a licensed psychologist, and has served as president of the Association of Mormon Counselors and Psychotherapists. He has published extensively in both Church history and psychology.

**Lloyd D. Newell** is Professor of Church History and Doctrine and holds the endowed Moral Education professorship at Brigham Young University. Since 1990 he has been the writer and narrator of the weekly *Music and the Spoken Word* broadcast of the Mormon Tabernacle Choir. He is the author of more than a dozen books.

**Neil K. Newell** is a prolific writer who has written plays, screenplays, novels, and his byline has appeared on more than 100 articles in national publications. A long-term employee of LDS Welfare Services, he also teaches a creative writing course at Brigham Young University in Provo, Utah.

**Craig J. Ostler,** Professor of Church History and Doctrine at Brigham Young University, has written or edited numerous articles and books on LDS doctrine and history, including *Salt Lake City: Ensign to the Nations.* He is an executive producer of videos and publications on LDS Church History sites and has a collection of thousands of photographs on Biblical lands, early LDS Church history, and current sites, many of which are available online at lds.org.

▼ *At times, everyone needs comfort from another person. Mormons believe "that when ye are in the service of your fellow beings ye are only in the service of your God" (Mosiah 2:17).*

**Carma T. Prete,** a former high school teacher, has had a sustained interest in baseball and astronomy. She has published articles on Latter-day Saint history in Ontario and more recently on grandparenting. She is the mother of six children and grandmother to 21.

**Roy A. Prete** is Emeritus Professor of Modern European and Canadian History at the Royal Military College of Canada, Kingston, Ontario. He is the editor or co-editor of six books, including *Window of Faith: Latter-day Saint Perspectives on World History,* and has published several articles and a volume on Anglo-French command relations in 1914—the first in a trilogy, with two more to come.

**Brent W. Roberts** is the managing director of the Meetinghouse Facilities Department for The Church of Jesus Christ of Latter-day Saints. His responsibilities include the acquisition of property, and the design, construction, and operation of Church meetinghouses throughout the world.

**Kip Sperry** is Professor of Church History and Doctrine at Brigham Young University. A well-known expert on genealogical research, he is the author of books, chapters, and articles and has lectured throughout the United States.

**Brent L. Top** is Professor of Church History and Doctrine at Brigham Young University and is currently the Department Chair. He also served as Associate Dean of Religious Education and held an endowed professorship in Moral Educations. He is the author or co-author of more than 20 books and numerous articles on the history, beliefs, and practices of Latter-day Saints.

**Helen K. Warner** has worked in public affairs, broadcasting, and won awards for historical research. She is actively involved in family and Church history and has published in several books and magazines. She has worked as a researcher for the Church History Museum in Salt Lake City and recently on the heritage designation of historical sites in Ontario, Canada.

**John W. Welch** holds a prestigious chair in the J. Reuben Clark Law School at Brigham Young University. He is the founder of the Foundation for Ancient Research and Mormon Studies and editor of *BYU Studies*. He is a leading scholar of Biblical and Latter-day Saint scriptures.

**Mary Jane Woodger,** Professor of Church History and Doctrine at Brigham Young University, is the author of twelve books and numerous articles. Her current research interests include 20th-century LDS Church history and Latter-day Saint women.

# Image Credits

# Index